KEO'S THAI CUISINE

Ten Speed Press

EDITOR	KEO SANANIKONE
RECIPE EDITOR AND FOOD STYLIST	BARBARA B. GRAY FOOD CONSULTANTS OF HAWAII
PHOTOGRAPHER	LEWIS HARRINGTON
GRAPHIC DESIGNERS	JOHN NAKAMA/DOUG CHUN
TYPESETTING	BESTYPE

All inquiries should be addressed to:
Keo Sananikone
Keo's Thai Cuisine
625 Kapahulu Avenue
Honolulu, Hawaii 96815
(808) 732-2593

TEN SPEED PRESS
P.O. Box 7123
Berkeley, California 94707

Library of Congress Cataloging-in-Publication Data
Keo Sananikone.
  Keo's Thai Cuisine.

  Includes index.
  1. Cookery, Thai. I. Title. II. Title: Thai Cuisine.
TX724.5 T5K46 1986   641.59593   86-14331
ISBN 0-89815-183-X

Printed in Singapore

ACKNOWLEDGEMENTS
I would like to extend my appreciation to all of my family and friends for their assistance, encouragement and invaluable support. And special thanks to Rujita Camba who taught me how to cook and Barbara Gray for her contribution to this book.

ABOUT THAI CUISINE

Thai cuisine is light, fresh and traditionally seasoned with chili peppers and aromatic herbs, a gourmet delight for those who know and love good food. It also has a temper. It can be as spicy hot (but not as heavy) as fiery Indian food or as gently flavored as Chinese. Happily, Thai cuisine is a pleasant contrast between the two. You can have it "spicy hot or spicy not." You decide.

The secret of Thai cooking is to maintain a delicate balance between the spices and main ingredients so that one does not overwhelm the other. Perfection comes with practice, and tasting; tasting is the key to success. Texture and color contrast is also important. These recipes will show you how.

Thai cuisine is amazingly versatile. One dish can have as many as seven or more variations. Although beef, chicken, pork and seafood are most often used, vegetarian dishes are equally popular. What a fine challenge for creative cooks.

Thai seasonings may seem complex. They're not. Many are your everyday favorites . . . garlic, onion, basil, coriander, ginger, mint, chili peppers, curry . . . plus Thai's own lemon grass, eggplant, kaffir lime leaves . . . It's the blend, the balance that counts . . . the magic that turns American fried chicken to Thai fried chicken. Exotic! Sophisticated! Delicious! It's all here!

And now to the kitchen.

coconut

dill

sweet basil

Eryngium
foetidum

Chine
parsle

Japanese eggplant

kra-chai
(lesser ginger)

ka
lin

Thai eggplant

kha
(Thai ginger)

common
ginger

kaffir

Thai eggplant

bamboo shoots

ong

shallots

Thai
papaya

dried
tamarind

Thai
papaya

chili
peppers

miniature
corn

dried chili
peppers

lemon grass

straw
mushrooms

CONTENTS

Commonly Used Ingredients 7

Utensils 12

RECIPES

    Appetizers 15

    Soups 35

    Salads 49

    Seafood, Poultry and Meat 61

    Vegetable Dishes 107

    Sauces and Pastes 117

    Curries 129

    Rice and Noodles 141

    Desserts 153

    Beverages 169

Garnish Ideas and Techniques 177

Thai Eating Habits 187

Menu Suggestions 188

Index 189

COMMONLY USED INGREDIENTS

bamboo shoots—
These are the edible shoots of certain bamboo plants. They are occasionally found fresh, as pictured, or more widely available in cans. They come in many varieties and sizes. Store leftover shoots in the refrigerator in water that is changed daily. They keep this way for about two weeks.

bananas—
There are about ten different varieties of bananas in Asia: apple, cooking, egg, Chinese, lady's finger, sweet, long, seeds, etc. They all come in different sizes, shapes, color and flavors. The most commonly used in Thai desserts are egg and apple bananas.

basil, sweet—
There are many varieties of basil. The most common are sweet basil, hot basil and lemon basil. Sweet basil has a flavor similar to anise. The hot and lemon basil have flavors closer to mint. Hot basil is stronger in flavor and is very popular for stir frying with meat among the Thais, but is not as commonly used by foreigners. Lemon basil is very popular in Laos and is used with dill in fish or chicken dishes.

bean sauce—
There are many new kinds of bean sauces. The most common ones are yellow, black and red bean sauce. Thai bean sauce is usually saltier than the Chinese or Japanese versions. In addition to beans the main ingredients are salt and sugar. Sauce is allowed to ferment.

bean threads—
Also commonly referred to as long rice, fun see and cellophane noodles. These are fine dried noodles made from mung bean flour. Sold in packets. They should be soaked for 15 to 30 minutes in warm water before using in a recipe. They have a transparent look after being soaked.

Chinese five spice powder—
This seasoning is a combination of ground fennel, star anise, ginger, licorice root, cinnamon and cloves.

Chinese parsley—
Chinese parsley is also called coriander or cilantro. The leaves, roots and seeds are used in Thai cooking. Each part has a unique flavor characteristic and use. The leaves are usually used for garnishing sauces, soups and salads. The roots are simmered in clear soup broths and used in fried chicken and meat by mixing with garlic, black pepper and salt. Only Thai cooking seems to use the seeds. They have a very strong taste and are usually found in curry pastes. The Thai name is pak-chee. It is the most widely used in Thai cooking. Chinese parsley is easy to grow. There is no substitute for flavor, but if used for garnish only, then parsley can be substituted.

chili peppers—
Chili peppers vary. The hottest are the very small chilies and the larger the milder. Mature chili are not always red. The seeds are the hottest part of the chili. What makes them "hot" is capsaicin concentrated in the seeds and the inside membranes. In preparing chili paste, milder dried whole chili is sometimes called for in recipes. Dried chili must be soaked in warm water for 5 minutes, then drained. Discard seeds. All immature peppers are green, but some mature green chili peppers never get red. If left on the plant they will turn yellow or red. Hot chili peppers dried and powdered produce cayenne. Milder red peppers are ground to produce paprika.

coconut—
Coconut milk is made by grating the flesh of a fresh coconut, then pouring warm water over it. The liquid extracted when this mixture is squeezed through a cloth is the coconut milk. Also available canned. Coconut milk gives body to sauces and gravies. It thickens when heated and has a sweet fragrance. It is a necessary ingredient in Thai curry dishes. Fresh coconuts contain coconut water, a popular chilled drink in Thailand.

corn, miniature—
Small baby corn available canned. An attractive addition to many dishes that need little or no cooking.

dill—
Dill is an annual of the parsley family. A medium sized herb with small feathery leaves and yellow flowers. Dill leaves can be chopped finely, fresh or dried, and sprinkled on soups, salads and seafoods. Sprigs of dill are used in their red chili fish and red curries. It has a clean odor faintly reminiscent of caraway, pungent and pleasantly aromatic.

eggplant, Japanese—
The long eggplant, sometimes called Japanese eggplant, is best used for stir fry dishes.

eggplant, Thai—
Sometimes served raw with a shrimp paste dip or cooked in a curry. They range from the size and shape of a pea to a cucumber or grapefruit. The pea size eggplants are used exclusively in Laos and Thailand. All varieties differ in color and size. They come in white, green, purple, yellow or mixed colors. White or yellow eggplants are popular among the Vietnamese and Laotians and widely used in making pickles. Pea size eggplants are bitter and are used mainly in sauces or in green curry dishes. Green peas can be substituted for these eggplants and would appeal more to Western taste.

eryngium foetidum—
The leaves of eryngium foetidum are used in salads and fish dishes. Vietnamese use them in their 'Pho' (noodle soup) as a garnish.

fish sauce—
This thin, translucent, salty brown sauce is an indispensable flavoring in Thai and Vietnamese cooking. It is made by salting down small fish that are packed in wooden barrels. The liquid that ''runs off'' is collected, cooked and bottled as fish sauce. The Vietnamese type is darker and generally more pungent than the Thai. Though the odor is strong when uncooked, the flavor mellows upon cooking. Fish sauce is milder in flavor than soy sauce and is often used in place of salt.

jackfruit—
This very sweet tropical fruit grown mainly in Southeast Asia and South America, but also in Hawaii. It grows on tree trunks and can reach the size of a watermelon.

ginger, common—
Also known as green ginger. It looks like a light brown-skinned gnarled root. When the thin skin is removed the flesh is sliced, shredded, chopped or grated. This ginger has a peppery, somewhat sweet flavor. Young ginger roots are plump, pale yellow and pink. They are often pickled, crystalized or made into a drink. Older ginger is more fibrous and much spicier and is obtainable year around.

ginger, Thai (kha, also known as laos)
This ginger is hard in texture. It has a lighter flesh and a slightly different flavor than common ginger. Northern Thais mix it in salads. Available in dried slides and as a powder. Sometimes called galangal. Fresh common ginger can be substituted for Kha.

ginger, lesser (Kra-chai)
The tubers of this ginger look like a bunch of brownish yellow fingers. Often added to fish curries or peeled and served as a raw vegetable.

kaffir lime leaves—

Thais use a great deal of kaffir lime and its leaves . . . in hot and sour lemon grass soup, curry pastes, sa-teh sauces and in stir fried dishes. Fresh kaffir lime and leaves are not available in many markets. Kaffir lime has been grown successfully in the Hawaiian Islands and is available in Honolulu at the Asian Grocery. Kaffir lime does not bear fruit until it is eight to ten years old. Grated zest of fresh lime can be used as a substitute in recipes calling for grated zest of kaffir limes. Kaffir lime leaves are used for flavor, like bay leaves, they should be removed from the dish before serving.

lemon grass—

Lemon grass is also called citronella and has a distinctive lemony flavor. The usual preparation method is to crush the lower part of the stalk and finely chop. Finely shredded lemon peel can be used as a substitute. The zest ½ lemon can be substituted for a stalk of lemon grass.

mint—

Thais use mint leaves in their salads, stir fried dishes and for garnishing. There are many different varieties of mint. If fresh mint is not available, simply omit it. Dried mint is not a good substitute.

mangoes—

Mangoes are big business in Thailand in both the export and domestic markets. They come in many varieties, sizes, colors and tastes—from fresh green and fresh ripe to pickled, dried and canned. Fresh mangoes are sold in Thailand movie lobbies, at open markets, in specialty stores and in restaurants. As a snack they are eaten with skin-on and dripping with a fish sauce mixed with roasted ground rice, sugar, chilies and sometimes shrimp paste. Late Spring through summer in Asia is definitely "mango times."

mushrooms, dried - Chinese black

The flavor of these dried mushrooms is distinctive. Sizes range from less than 1-inch to about 2-inches in diameter. They keep indefinitely when stored in tightly covered containers. Before using they must be soaked in warm water for 15 to 30 minutes. The best should be reserved for dishes in which the mushrooms are cooked whole. Less expensive mushrooms are perfect for recipes calling for slicing or quartering. Fresh mushrooms can be substituted, but are not as flavorful.

mushrooms, straw—

These are thin, leaflike mushrooms available fresh or canned. They have a wonderful texture and should be used as soon as possible after the can is opened. An attractive addition to many dishes, they need little or no cooking. If not available, use small, fresh mushrooms.

noodles, rice—

There are a variety of sizes. Those made from sticky rice are sometimes referred to as rice sticks. Very fine strands made from long grain rice are often called rice vermicelli noodles. Before using in a dish, rice noodles are usually presoaked in warm water. For a crisp garnish or appetizer fry rice noodles a small amount at a time in hot oil. They puff up and whiten instantly.

ong choi—

The Thai name for this vegetable is pak-boong. This green, smooth leafed vegetable has a flavor milder than spinach and a texture similar to watercress.

oyster sauce—
A thickened brown sauce of oyster juices and salt. Used both as a flavoring and a condiment. Usually, the more expensive the sauce, the better the quality. It can be stored for a long time in the refrigerator.

palm sugar—
A coarse brown sugar, sold in lumps or cakes. It is made from the sap of the Palmyra palm and is used as a sweetener. Dark brown sugar can be substituted.

papaya, thai—
Papayas come in many varieties in Thailand and range in size and shape from about 5-inches to 30-inches in length. The green papaya is popular in Northeastern Thailand and Laos. Thai green papaya salad comes mixed with long string beans and anchovy; dried shrimp powder, sugar and ground peanuts; raw pickled crabs and anchovy. Some use plain papaya with tomatoes, garlic, lime juice and fish sauce. The ripe papaya is commonly served chilled as a dessert.

radish, pickled salted—
Fresh white radish is sun dried, then salted and stored about one month before use. No refrigeration is required for the dark brown pickled radish. Use sparingly because it is very salty.

rice, brown—
This is rice that has been hulled but not lost its bran, brown rice contains more nutrients than polished white rice.

rice, sweet—
A short grain rice, quite sticky when cooked. Also called glutinous rice or sticky rice. Used in a number of thai dessert recipes.

rice flour—
This is rice ground to a very fine powder. Often used as a coating before ingredients are deep fried.

rice papers—
These round, paper-thin wrappers are made primarily from sticky rice. After being formed the rice papers are dried. Dampen with water before use to make them pliable and ready for filling.

shallots—
Shallots are a small, brown-skinned member of the onion family. These slender, pear-shaped bulbs are intense in taste without being unduly pungent. They grow singly or in clusters and are more seasonal than onions. Shallots taste sweet and delicate and they are mostly used for flavoring. When recipes specify shallots, they should be used. Browning makes shallots taste a little bitter. The white part of the scallion is an acceptable substitute.

Sriracha sauce—
This Thai style pepper sauce is made from chili peppers, salt, sugar and vinegar. Not only hot and sour, but also sweet. Available in bottles in most Asian markets.

tamarind—
Tamarind comes in green, ripe, dried, preserved, canned or liquid form. It has an acidic taste with a little sweet and sour flavor. Both the pulp and young tiny leaves are edible. Dried tamarind pulp can be soaked in warm water for 10 minutes. Squeeze the pulp into the water, then strain. Use the water in recipes. The longer the tamarind soaks the stronger the flavor of the liquid.

tofu—

Tofu is a soft white cake of pressed soybean curd. It is bland in taste, but absorbs the flavor and aroma of ingredients with which it is mixed. Considered the finest known source of low cost, high quality protein. It is low in saturated fats and calories and totally free of cholesterol. If not used right away, store in the refrigerator in water that is changed daily. Will keep for about five days. Tofu is also available pressed, deep fried and in dried sheets.

shrimp paste—

Thick paste with greyish color and a very strong odor. If kept stored in a tightly closed jar in the refrigerator, it keeps indefinitely. Anchovy paste may be substituted.

soy sauce—

Made from soy beans, flour, salt and water. Light soy sauces are lighter in color and thinner in consistency and are saltier than dark soy sauces. Dark soy sauce, or black soy sauce as they are often labeled, are sweetened with molasses. They are occasionally labeled "double dark" to indicate deeper color and strength. Use light soys for shrimp, chicken and pork; darker soys with red meats, for roasting, or for richer color in sauces. If too salty, dilute with water.

If you have difficulty in finding any of these ingredients in your local markets, please write or call:

ASIAN GROCERY
1319 South Beretania Street
Honolulu, Hawaii 96814
Telephone (808) 531-8371 or (808) 536-7440

1. Bamboo Steamer Basket
2. Aluminum Steamer for Sticky Rice
3. Stock Pot
4. Aluminum Steamed Rice Server
5. Clay Mortar
6. Wooden Pestle
7. Bamboo Basket Sticky Rice Server
8. 3-Tiered Aluminum Steamer
9. Soup Server (with center section for hot charcoal)
10. Sauce Pot
11. Cleaver

Woks are used in China and throughout Southeast Asia. The unique shape of the wok allows for rapid stir frying. This cooking method uses tossing motions when cooking in a small amount of oil over high heat to seal in flavors.

Woks are made from many different materials, the best being thin cast iron that gives very even heat. Cast iron woks should be seasoned well before using for the first time or reseasoned if they have to be scoured to remove rust or food. Rinse the wok and dry well. Rub with oil and heat to a high temperature; cool. Repeat this process until a shiny smooth glaze has formed on the inside of the wok. From this time on all you need to do is wipe it out, rinse if necessary, dry well and return to heat to evaporate any moisture that may still be left.

APPETIZERS

Keo's Thai Spring Rolls — 17
Fish Patties — 18
Shrimp Rolls — 19
Crisp Noodles — 21
Stuffed Tofu — 22
Bangkok Stuffed Wings — 23
Crispy Fried Crab Claws — 26
Crispy Fried Chicken — 27
Sa-teh On Skewers — 29
Son-In-Law Eggs — 30
Salted Eggs — 31
Crisp Fried Tofu — 33

A highly recommended appetizer at all of Keo's restaurants. These small delicacies of pork, shrimp, mushrooms, long rice and spices are wrapped in crispy rice paper and served with fresh lettuce and mint leaves. Take the lettuce leaf, add some mint, a slice of cucumber, a spring roll and a dollop of sauce. Two to three bites and you have an excellent Thai experience.

KEO'S THAI SPRING ROLLS

(Illustrated on opposite page)

½	**pound fresh ground pork**
¼	**pound shrimp or crabmeat, chopped**
10	**dried Chinese black mushrooms**
1	**ounce bean threads**
1	**medium onion, finely chopped**
1	**carrot, shredded**
¼	**pound bean sprouts**
½	**teaspoon ground black pepper**
1 to 2	**teaspoons fish sauce* or ½ teaspoon salt**
1	**teaspoon sugar**
1	**cup lukewarm water**
12	**rice papers, quartered**
6	**cups oil for deep frying**
48	**lettuce leaves**
1	**bunch fresh mint**
1	**cucumber, thinly sliced**
	Spring Roll Sauce (recipe page 120)

In a medium bowl combine pork and shrimp. Soak mushrooms in warm water for 20 minutes; remove stems and chop caps. Soak bean threads in warm water for 20 minutes, then cut into 1-inch lengths. Add mushrooms, bean threads, onion, carrot, bean sprouts, black pepper and fish sauce to pork mixture; mix well. Set mixture aside for 15 minutes to allow flavors of ingredients to blend. Dilute sugar in lukewarm water. Place rice paper on a flat surface and brush with water until it is pliable. Place 2 teaspoons of filling near the edge of the rice paper, then fold rice paper over the filling. Fold the right side over to enclose filling, then fold over left side. Continue to roll, then seal. Heat oil for deep frying to 375F. Deep fry a few rolls at a time until crisp and golden brown, about 15 minutes. Fry the remaining rolls. Serve by placing a spring roll in a lettuce leaf and top with mint and cucumber slices. Serve with Spring Roll Sauce. Accompany with chili sauce and chopped peanuts, if desired. Makes 48 to 55.

Technique for WRAPPING SPRING ROLLS (refer to page 184)

*The amount of fish sauce used in this recipe depends on the brand selected and personal taste.

Fish Patties, sometimes called fish cake in Thailand, is a very popular appetizer usually accompanied with a chilled Thai beer. Fresh opakapaka or other firm white fish is finely minced and blended with string beans and Thai spices. Deep fry and serve with Cucumber Sauce for dipping.

FISH PATTIES

½	pound firm white fish filet
3	ounces fresh string beans, finely chopped
1	onion, finely chopped
1	stalk fresh lemon grass, finely chopped
1	tablespoon finely chopped Chinese parsley
1 to 2	teaspoons seeded and finely chopped red chili peppers
1 to 2	tablespoons fish sauce*
1	egg
2	tablespoons cornstarch
¼	teaspoon sugar
5	cups oil for deep frying
	Cucumber Sauce (recipe page 121)

Mince fish filet. Combine fish, string beans, onion, lemon grass, Chinese parsley, red chili peppers, fish sauce, egg, cornstarch and sugar; blend well. Preheat oil for deep frying to medium heat. Shape fish mixture into patties 2-inches in diameter and ½-inch thick. Fry 10 to 15 minutes or until golden brown. Drain on absorbent paper towels. Serve with Cucumber Sauce. Makes 4 to 6 servings.

*The amount of fish sauce used in this recipe depends on the brand selected and personal taste.

Shrimp Rolls are very similar to Spring Rolls, except that they are wrapped in tofu sheets instead of rice papers. Steam first before deep frying. Usually an hors d'oeuvre, but they can be served as a main course.

SHRIMP ROLLS

12	large sheets dried tofu
1	pound shrimp
2	ounces crabmeat, chopped
1	ounce ground pork
1 to 2	ounces Chinese parsley sprigs, finely chopped
2	cloves garlic, finely chopped
½	teaspoon finely chopped common ginger
2	tablespoons cornstarch
1 to 2	teaspoons fish sauce* or ½ teaspoon salt
¼	teaspoon ground black pepper
5	cups oil for deep frying
	Spring Roll Sauce (recipe page 120) or
	Sriracha sauce

Soak tofu sheets in warm water for 15 minutes to soften, then drain and set aside individual sheets on a flat surface. Shell and devein shrimp; finely chop. Combine shrimp, crab, pork, Chinese parsley, garlic, ginger, cornstarch, fish sauce and black pepper; blend well. Shape shrimp mixture into cylinders and place on tofu sheets; roll up. Steam for 15 minutes, then set aside to cool. Preheat oil for deep frying to medium heat. Deep fry for 10 to 12 minutes or until golden brown. Drain on absorbent paper towels. Slice each roll crosswise and serve with Spring Roll Sauce or Sriracha sauce. Makes 4 to 6 servings.

*The amount of fish sauce   used in this recipe depends on the brand selected and personal taste.

The original Thai dish. Crisp and sweet small noodles that will melt in your mouth. Tossed with diced chicken and shrimp and flavorful tamarind sauce. An excellent introduction to Thai cuisine.

CRISP NOODLES

(Illustrated on opposite page)

¼	**pound boneless chicken breast**
2	**ounces shrimp (optional)**
½	**cup dried tamarind**
½	**cup warm water**
1	**teaspoon catsup**
1 to 4	**tablespoons fish sauce***
1	**tablespoon red wine vinegar**
⅓	**cup brown sugar**
5	**cups oil for deep frying**
½	**cup bean sprouts**
1	**green onion, chopped**
4	**ounces rice noodles**
Garnish:	**4 to 5 sprigs Chinese parsley**
	Red chili flowers (directions page 179)

Dice chicken. Shell and devein shrimp; dice. Combine tamarind and warm water; blend well and strain. In a large saucepan combine chicken, shrimp, tamarind water, catsup, fish sauce, wine vinegar and brown sugar; bring to a boil over high heat. Immediately reduce heat to low and simmer for 1 hour. Set sauce aside to cool. In a wok heat oil for deep frying on high heat. Fry rice noodles; a little at a time, until they puff up. Place noodles on absorbent paper towels to drain. Combine noodles, sauce, bean sprouts and green onion; toss lightly to mix. Garnish with Chinese parsley and red chili peppers. Serve immediately, since noodles soften within 10 minutes after combining with sauce. Makes 6 to 8 servings.

*The amount of fish sauce used in this recipe depends on the brand selected and personal taste.

Tofu, also called bean curd or bean cake, is made from soy beans and is available in many forms. This recipe uses deep-fried tofu cubes that are stuffed with a flavorful pork mixture.

STUFFED TOFU

6	ounces ground lean pork
2	cloves garlic, finely chopped
¼	cup chopped green onions
2	tablespoons chopped Chinese parsley
¼	teaspoon salt
$1/_8$	teaspoon black pepper
1	teaspoon cornstarch
8	pieces (approximately 4 ounces each) deep-fried tofu
2	cups oil for deep frying
	Spring Roll Sauce (recipe page 120)
Garnish:	Red chili pepper
	Chinese parsley sprigs

In a large bowl combine pork, garlic, green onions, chopped Chinese parsley, salt, black pepper and cornstarch; blend well. Make a hole in each tofu cube with the tip of a knife and stuff the pork mixture into the opening. Heat oil on medium and deep fry stuffed tofu until golden brown. Drain on absorbent paper towels. Serve with spring roll sauce. Garnish with red chili pepper and Chinese parsley sprigs. Serve hot. Makes 4 servings.

These deboned chicken wings are filled with a beautiful blend of chicken, mushrooms, carrots, long rice, onion, waterchestnuts and spices. They can be steamed and frozen, ready to deep fry golden brown just before serving.

BANGKOK STUFFED WINGS

4	**pounds chicken wings**
1	**pound shrimp**
1	**ounce bean threads**
2	**carrots, shredded**
¼	**cup water chestnuts**
1	**onion**
2 to 4	**tablespoons fish sauce* or 1 teaspoon salt**
2 to 3	**cloves garlic**
¼	**teaspoon ground black pepper**
1	**tablespoon Chinese parsley roots**
1	**cup rice flour or cornstarch**
5	**cups oil for deep frying**
	Sa-teh Sauce (recipe page 119) or Sriracha sauce

Debone chicken wings according to method shown on page 185. Shell and devein shrimp. Soak bean threads in warm water for 15 minutes; drain and cut into 1-inch lengths. In a food processor combine chicken meat obtained from deboning, shrimp, carrots, water chestnuts, onion, fish sauce, garlic, black pepper and Chinese parsley roots; blend until smooth. Stir in bean threads. Stuff chicken mixture loosely into the wings. Steam about 20 minutes or until almost cooked. They can be frozen at this point and deep fried when ready to serve. Coat wings with rice flour. Heat oil for deep frying to 375F. Deep fry wings until golden brown. Serve warm with Sa-teh Sauce or Sriracha sauce. Makes 6 to 8 servings.

Technique for DEBONING CHICKEN WINGS (refer to page 185)

*The amount of fish sauce used in this recipe depends on the brand selected and personal taste.

These crab claws with a crispy coating of rice flour, lemon grass, and red chilies make a delicious appetizer.

CRISP FRIED CRAB CLAWS

(Illustrated on pages 24 and 25)

8	large crab claws
¼	cup rice flour
2	tablespoons cornstarch
½	teaspoon sugar or honey
1	stalk fresh lemon grass, finely chopped
4	cloves garlic, finely chopped
1	tablespoon finely chopped Chinese parsley
1 to 2	teaspoons seeded and finely chopped red chili peppers (optional)
1	teaspoon soy sauce
1	egg
1 to 2	teaspoons fish sauce* or ½ teaspoon salt
¼	teaspoon black pepper
¼	cup cold water
5	cups oil for deep frying
	Spring Roll Sauce (recipe page 120)
Garnish:	Lettuce leaves (optional)

Rinse crab claws and pat dry. Combine rice flour, cornstarch, sugar, lemon grass, garlic, Chinese parsley, red chili peppers, soy sauce, egg, fish sauce and black pepper; blend well. Stir in cold water and mix well. Preheat oil for deep frying on medium heat. Coat crab claws with rice flour mixture. Deep fry for 12 to 15 minutes or until golden brown. Drain on absorbent paper towels. Serve with Spring Roll Sauce. Garnish with lettuce leaves. Makes 4 servings.

*The amount of fish sauce used in this recipe depends on the brand selected and personal taste.

This is an Eurasian dish found mainly in Bangkok's Western-style restaurants.

CRISPY FRIED CHICKEN

>   2   pounds chicken wings (drummettes)
>   3   stalks fresh lemon grass, finely chopped
>   1   ounce garlic, peeled and finely chopped
>   (about 6 large cloves)
> 2 to 4   tablespoons fish sauce* or
>   2 teaspoons salt
>   2   teaspoons brown sugar
>   ½   teaspoon ground black pepper
>   2   tablespoons oil
>   3   tablespoons rice flour
>   3   tablespoons chopped Chinese parsley roots
>   3   cups oil for deep frying
>   Spring Roll Sauce (recipe page 120) or
>   Sriracha sauce

In a bowl combine chicken, lemon grass, garlic, fish sauce, brown sugar, black pepper, oil, rice flour and Chinese parsley roots; mix well. Marinate beef in the refrigerator overnight. In a wok heat the oil for deep frying on medium heat until oil is hot. Place the chicken, piece by piece, in the oil and fry until dry and cooked, about 15 minutes. Remove chicken; drain thoroughly on absorbent paper towels. Let cool before serving. Serve at room temperature with Spring Roll Sauce, if desired. Makes 6 to 8 servings.

*The amount of fish sauce used in this recipe depends on the brand selected and personal taste.

Sa-teh originally was an Indonesian specialty. You will find the Thai version a little bit spicier than the Indonesian.

SA-TEH ON SKEWERS

(Illustrated on opposite page)

1	**pound combination of boneless chicken, beef and pork**
3	**tablespoons oil**
1	**stalk fresh lemon grass**
3	**cloves garlic**
½	**teaspoon seeded and finely chopped red chili peppers**
1	**tablespoon curry powder**
1	**teaspoon sugar or honey**
½ to 1	**teaspoon fish sauce* or ¼ teaspoon salt**
	Skewers
	Sa-teh Sauce (recipe page 119)
	Cucumber Sauce (recipe page 121)

Cut chicken, beef and pork thinly into 2-inch strips. In a food processor or blender combine oil, lemon grass, garlic, red chili peppers, curry powder, sugar and fish sauce; blend until smooth. Pour over chicken and meat; marinate for two hours. Thread meat onto skewers and barbecue or broil, turning occasionally, until cooked. Serve with Sa-teh Sauce and Cucumber Sauce. Makes 4 servings.

*The amount of fish sauce used in this recipe depends on the brand selected and personal taste.

Son-in-law eggs is a direct translation of the Thai name for this dish. These are hard boiled eggs deep fried and covered with a sweet palm sugar sauce.

SON-IN-LAW EGGS

6	**hard boiled eggs**
2	**cups oil**
4	**shallots, finely chopped**
2	**cloves garlic, finely chopped**
2	**tablespoons palm sugar or brown sugar**
¼	**cup hot water**
1 to 2	**teaspoons fish sauce***
4	**lettuce leaves**
Garnish:	**Chinese parsley sprigs**
	Green onions, cut into 2-inch lengths

Peel hard boiled eggs. Heat oil in a wok on medium heat and deep fry eggs until golden brown. Set eggs aside to cool for 20 minutes, then cut eggs into quarters. In 1 tablespoon of the oil stir fry shallots and garlic until golden brown; drain on absorbent paper towels. In a saucepan dissolve palm sugar in hot water; add fish sauce and mix well for 3 minutes. Stir in shallots and garlic. To serve, arrange lettuce leaves on a large platter and top with egg quarters and pour sauce over the top. Garnish with Chinese parsley and green onions. Makes 3 servings.

*The amount of fish sauce used in this recipe depends on the brand selected and personal taste.

There are villages in Thailand where refrigeration is not available so farmers preserve their meat, poultry, seafood, vegetables and eggs by methods of pickling, salting, drying or fermenting. Today, these delicacies are very much in demand in gourmet stores and markets in Thailand cities.

SALTED EGGS

2   **cups salt**
4   **cups hot water**
12 **eggs**

In a one-gallon glass jar dissolve salt in hot water; set aside to cool. Place eggs into the salt water; cover with a tight fitting lid and let soak for six weeks. After six weeks, drain off salt water. Hard boil all the eggs and refrigerate. Keep shells on until ready to serve.

"French fried" fresh tofu served with a spicy Spring Roll Sauce, Sa-teh Sauce, crisp lettuce and cool, refreshing cucumber slices. A delightful appetizer.

CRISP FRIED TOFU

(Illustrated on opposite page)

½	**pound tofu**
¼	**cup rice flour**
2	**tablespoons cornstarch**
5	**cups oil for deep frying**
	Spring Roll Sauce (recipe page 120)
	Sa-teh Sauce (recipe page 119)
	Lettuce leaves
	Cucumber slices
Garnish:	**Chinese parsley sprigs**

Cut tofu into strips 2 x 1 x ¼-inches. Combine rice flour and cornstarch. Preheat oil for deep frying on medium heat. Coat tofu with rice flour mixture. Deep fry for 7 to 10 minutes or until golden brown. Drain on absorbent paper towels. Serve with Spring Roll Sauce, Sa-teh Sauce, lettuce leaves and cucumber slices. Garnish with Chinese parsley. Makes 3 to 4 servings.

SOUPS

Spicy Shrimp Soup with Lemon Grass — 37
Thai Ginger Chicken Soup — 38
Thai Soup Stock — 39
Rice Soup — 42
Thai Chicken Soup with Bean Threads — 43
Thai Noodle Soup with Beef Meatballs — 45
Egg Noodle Soup with Char Siu — 46
Thai Noodle Soup with Chicken — 47

The most popular soup in Thailand. A classic Thai seafood soup of excellent taste. Minutes quick for easy preparation. Lemon grass and kaffir lime leaves are there for flavor, but not to be eaten.

SPICY SHRIMP SOUP WITH LEMON GRASS

(Illustrated on opposite page)

½ **pound shrimp**
4 **cups water**
1 **stalk fresh lemon grass, sliced**
1 **can (8 oz.) straw mushrooms, drained**
2 **kaffir lime leaves**
1 to 4 **tablespoons fish sauce***
¼ **cup fresh lime juice**
2 **tablespoons sliced green onions**
1 **tablespoon chopped Chinese parsley**
1 to 4 **red chili peppers, seeded and chopped or ½ teaspoon red chili paste**
Garnish: **Chinese parsley sprigs**

Devein shrimp; leave shells on for color, if desired. Bring water to a boil. Add lemon grass and straw mushrooms; immediately reduce heat to medium-low. Add shrimp and cook for 3 minutes; stir in fish sauce and lime juice. Sprinkle with green onions, Chinese parsley and red chili peppers, if desired. Serve hot. Garnish with Chinese parsley sprigs. Makes 4 servings.

Note: Fresh mushrooms can be substituted for the canned mushrooms, but add at end of cooking time.

Idea: Spicy Thai Vegetable Soup can be prepared by substituting tofu and mixed vegetables (refer to page 81) for the shrimp. Use ½ teaspoon of salt instead of the fish sauce.

*The amount of fish sauce used in this recipe depends on the brand selected and personal taste.

Thai ginger with tender slices of light chicken meat simmered in coconut milk with green onions and spices. Mild.

THAI GINGER CHICKEN SOUP

½	**pound boneless chicken breast**
3	**cups coconut milk**
2	**cups water**
1-inch	**section kha (Thai ginger), thinly sliced**
1 to 4	**tablespoons fish sauce***
¼	**cup fresh lime juice**
2	**tablespoons sliced green onions**
1	**tablespoon chopped Chinese parsley**
Garnish:	**1 to 3 red chili peppers, seeded and slivered**
	Chinese parsley sprigs

Cut chicken into thin strips. Bring coconut milk and water to a boil. Reduce heat to medium-low; add chicken and cook for 3 minutes. Stir in Thai ginger, fish sauce and lime juice. Sprinkle with green onions and Chinese parsley. Serve hot. Garnish with red chili peppers and Chinese parsley sprigs. Makes 4 servings.

Note: Fresh common ginger can be substituted for kha.

*The amount of fish sauce used in this recipe depends on the brand selected and personal taste.

Rice and noodle soups often are considered as a full meal in Thailand and are derived from Chinese. In fact, the Thai words for noodles "gway-tio, mee" are Chinese. Soups vary greatly depending on the main ingredients and soup stock. Cooked rice or noodles are added along with various garnishings.

THAI SOUP STOCK

6 **cups water**
1 **pound chicken bones, beef bones or white radish for a vegetarian stock**
1-inch **section common ginger, thinly sliced**
4 to 5 **Chinese parsley roots**
1 **whole onion, quartered**
1 **teaspoon salt**

In a stockpot bring water to a boil. Add chicken bones, ginger, Chinese parsley roots, onion and salt. Reduce heat and simmer for ½ hour. Strain stock and reserve for use in the following soups.

Rice soup in Thailand is usually spicier and thinner than the Chinese version.

RICE SOUP

(Illustrated on pages 40 and 41)

5	**cups Thai Soup Stock (recipe page 39)**
¼	**cup minced beef, chicken, pork, fish or shrimp**
1	**tablespoon minced common ginger**
2½	**cups cooked rice**
1 to 2	**tablespoons fish sauce***
1	**egg**
Garnish:	**2 green onions, finely chopped**
	1 tablespoon chopped Chinese parsley
	1 tablespoon onion or garlic flakes
	1 teaspoon dried red chili pepper flakes (optional)

In a stockpot heat Thai Soup Stock. Add minced meat or seafood and ginger; bring to a boil, stirring occasionally. Reduce heat to simmer. Add rice and cook for 2 minutes. Season with fish sauce. Break egg into a serving bowl and beat lightly. Pour soup on top of the egg. Garnish with green onions, Chinese parsley, onion flakes and red chili flakes. Serve hot. Makes 6 servings.

*The amount of fish sauce used in this recipe depends on the brand selected and personal taste.

This very mild chicken soup with bean thread is popular among the Chinese Thai.

THAI CHICKEN SOUP WITH BEAN THREADS

(Illustrated on page 41)

¼	**pound bean threads**
½	**pound boneless chicken breast**
5	**cups Thai Soup Stock (recipe page 39)**
1	**can (8 oz.) straw mushrooms, drained**
1	**can (8 oz.) miniature corn, drained**
1	**can (5 oz.) water chestnuts, thinly sliced**
¼	**cup shredded bamboo shoots**
2	**stalks green onions, cut into 2-inch lengths**
Garnish:	**Chinese parsley sprigs**

Soak bean threads in warm water for 15 minutes; drain. Shred chicken. Bring soup stock to a boil. Add chicken, bean threads, straw mushrooms, miniature corn, water chestnuts, bamboo shoots and green onions. Reduce heat and simmer 3 to 5 minutes. Garnish with Chinese parsley. Makes 6 servings.

This Thai noodle soup with meatballs is a popular snack, particularly among the students.

THAI NOODLE SOUP WITH BEEF MEATBALLS

(Illustrated on opposite page)

¼	pound rice noodles
5	cups Thai Soup Stock
½	pound beef meatballs or shredded beef
2	ounces fresh bean sprouts
1 to 2	teaspoons fish sauce
Garnish:	Chinese parsley sprigs
	2 tablespoons chopped green onions
	1 teaspoon chopped fresh red chili peppers or ground red chili peppers

Soak rice noodles in warm water for 15 minutes; drain. Bring stock to a boil. Add rice noodles, meatballs, bean sprouts and fish sauce. Reduce heat and simmer for 5 to 7 minutes. Garnish with Chinese parsley sprigs, green onions and red chili peppers. Makes 6 servings.

A. THAI NOODLE SOUP WITH BEEF MEATBALLS
B. EGG NOODLE SOUP WITH CHAR SIU
C. THAI NOODLE SOUP WITH CHICKEN
D. EGG NOODLES
E. RICE NOODLES

Clockwise from top left: Thai Noodle Soup with Beef Meatballs, Thai Noodle Soup with Chicken (page 47), and Egg Noodle Soup with Char Siu (page 46)

Egg noodle soup with clear char siu is more popular among city folks than the villagers.

EGG NOODLE SOUP WITH CHAR SIU

(Illustrated on page 44)

½	pound char siu (Chinese barbecued pork)
5	cups Thai Soup Stock (recipe page 39)
¼	pound egg noodles
2	ounces bean sprouts
1 to 2	teaspoons fish sauce*
Garnish:	Chinese parsley sprigs
2	tablespoons chopped green onions
1	teaspoon dried red chili pepper flakes (optional)

Thinly slice char siu. Bring stock to a boil. Add noodles, char siu, bean sprouts and fish sauce. Reduce heat and simmer for 3 to 5 minutes. Garnish with Chinese parsley sprigs, green onions and red chili pepper flakes. Makes 3 to 4 servings.

*The amount of fish sauce used in this recipe depends on the brand selected and personal taste.

Boneless chicken and fresh bean sprouts make this a nice variation of Thai noodle soup.

THAI NOODLE SOUP WITH CHICKEN

(illustrated on page 44)

¼	**pound rice noodles**
5	**cups Thai Soup Stock (recipe page 39)**
½	**pound boneless chicken breast**
2	**ounces bean sprouts**
1 to 2	**teaspoons fish sauce***
Garnish:	**Chinese parsley sprigs**
	2 tablespoons chopped green onions
	1 teaspoon seeded and chopped red chili peppers or ground red chili peppers (optional)

Soak rice noodles in warm water for 15 minutes; drain. Bring stock to a boil. Add rice noodles, chicken, bean sprouts and fish sauce. Reduce heat and simmer for 5 to 7 minutes. Garnish with Chinese parsley sprigs, green onions and red chili peppers. Makes 3 to 6 servings.

*The amount of fish sauce used in this recipe depends on the brand selected and personal taste.

SALADS

Chieng Mai Chicken Salad — 51
Cucumber Salad — 52
Thai Beef Salad — 53
Calamari Salad with Fresh Lemon Grass — 55
Young Green Tamarind Salad — 56
Green Papaya Salad — 57

Chieng Mai is a northeastern city in Thailand, culturally very close to Laos, and famous for its chicken salad which was originally called "laap". Laotians make their laap with beef, chicken or pork using the liver, gizzard, tripe and skin. Uncooked fresh water fish and shrimp with anchovy and lime juice are other variations.

CHIENG MAI CHICKEN SALAD

(Illustrated on opposite page)

1	pound boneless chicken, ground
1	stalk fresh lemon grass, finely chopped
3	kaffir lime leaves, finely chopped
3 to 6	red chili peppers, seeded and chopped (optional)
¼	cup fresh lime juice
1 to 2	tablespoons fish sauce*
1	tablespoon ground roasted rice**
1	green onion, chopped
6 to 8	sprigs Chinese parsley, chopped
12	mint leaves, chopped
1	teaspoon ground red chili peppers (optional)
	Lettuce leaves or cabbage squares
Garnish:	Green onions, sliced
	Mint leaves

Heat a small skillet and cook chicken in a little water, but without oil, stirring constantly. Set chicken aside to cool. In a bowl combine chicken, lemon grass, kaffir lime leaves, chopped red chili peppers, lime juice and fish sauce; mix well. Stir in ground roasted rice, green onion, chopped Chinese parsley and chopped mint leaves. Transfer to a platter and serve at room temperature with lettuce leaves. Garnish with green onions and mint leaves. Makes 6 servings.

*The amount of fish sauce used in this recipe depends on the brand selected and personal taste.

**To prepare ground roasted rice place rice in heavy pan over medium heat. Carefully brown the rice until very dark brown. Set aside to cool. Place in blender or spice mill and reduce to a fine powder. Store in an airtight container.

This cucumber salad is one of the favorite noontime snacks for farmers.

CUCUMBER SALAD

2	large cucumbers
2	red chili peppers, seeded and chopped
1	clove garlic, minced
½ to 1	tablespoon fish sauce* or anchovy paste
2 to 3	tablespoons fresh lime juice
½	teaspoon ground dried shrimp

Shred cucumbers. In a large bowl combine shredded cucumber and all the remaining ingredients; toss lightly to mix. Serve immediately to prevent ingredients from marinating. Makes 4 servings.

Note: Long string beans cut into 2-inch strips can be substituted for the shredded cucumbers.

*The amount of fish sauce used in this recipe depends on the brand selected and personal taste.

A spicy dressing tossed with thinly sliced strips of cooked roast beef and other classic Thai ingredients . . . results are superb and very popular.

THAI BEEF SALAD

(Illustrated on page 54)

1	**pound cooked roast beef**
¼	**ounce bean threads**
1	**onion, thinly sliced**
1	**small cucumber, thinly sliced**
1	**stalk fresh lemon grass, thinly sliced**
¼	**cup fresh lime juice**
1 to 2	**tablespoons fish sauce***
2 to 4	**red chili peppers, seeded and chopped (optional)**
10 to 15	**mint leaves**
2	**green onions, chopped**
Garnish:	**Green onion brushes (directions page 183)**
	Lime
	Radish roses (optional)
	Mint leaves

Thinly slice roast beef into 2-inch strips. Soak bean threads in warm water for 15 minutes; drain and cut into 3-inch lengths. In a large bowl combine roast beef, bean threads, onion, cucumber, lemon grass, lime juice, fish sauce, red chili peppers, mint leaves and chopped green onions; toss to mix well. Garnish with green onion brushes, lime, radish roses and mint leaves. Serve chilled or near room temperature. Makes 6 servings.

*The amount of fish sauce used in this recipe depends on the brand selected and personal taste.

Calamari dishes are very popular in Southern Thailand and Bangkok. Calamari is available fresh, frozen, dried and pickled. Fresh calamari is best for salads, but frozen is acceptable. All Thai salads are served chilled or near room temperature and are prepared just before serving to prevent dressing from marinating the main ingredients.

CALAMARI SALAD WITH FRESH LEMON GRASS

(Illustrated on opposite page)

1	pound calamari (squid)
¼	ounce bean threads
⅓	cup water
1	stalk fresh lemon grass, finely chopped
3	fresh kaffir lime leaves, finely chopped
1	onion, thinly sliced
5	teaspoons fresh lime juice
½ to 1	tablespoon fish sauce*
1 to 5	red chili peppers, seeded and chopped (optional)
15 to 20	mint leaves
6 to 8	sprigs Chinese parsley, chopped
1	green onion, finely chopped
3 to 5	lettuce leaves (optional)
Garnish:	Red chili flowers (directions page 179)
	Lime

Rinse calamari well in cold water. Soak bean threads in warm water for 15 minutes; drain and cut into 3-inch lengths. Prepare calamari according to technique on page 186. In a small saucepan bring water to a boil and add calamari. Cook for 3 to 5 minutes or until opaque; drain. Set aside for a few minutes to cool. Combine lemon grass, kaffir lime leaves, onion, lime juice, fish sauce and red chili peppers. Just before serving combine calamari, dressing, bean threads, mint, chopped Chinese parsley and green onion; toss to mix well. Serve with lettuce leaves, if desired. Garnish with red chili pepper flowers and lime. Serve chilled or near room temperature. Makes 6 servings.

Technique for CLEANING AND SCORING SQUID (refer to page 186)

*The amount of fish sauce used in this recipe depends on the brand selected and personal taste.

Top: Calamari Salad with Fresh Lemon Grass (page 55)
Bottom: Thai Beef Salad (page 53)

Young green tamarind with its soft seeds are pounded in a mortar with red chili peppers, shallots, sugar and a touch of shrimp paste. An original Thai salad!

YOUNG GREEN TAMARIND SALAD

½ **pound young green tamarind, rinsed and chopped**
2 **shallots, peeled and chopped**
2 to 6 **red chili peppers, chopped**
1 **teaspoon palm sugar or honey**
¹/₈ **teaspoon shrimp paste or fish sauce**
Lettuce leaves or cabbage squares

Combine young green tamarind, shallots, red chili peppers, palm sugar and shrimp paste in a mortar and pound them together for ½ minute. Serve with lettuce leaves, if desired. Makes 3 to 4 servings.

A packet-type salad easy to make, fun to eat.

GREEN PAPAYA SALAD

(Illustrated on pages 58 and 59)

½	**pound green papaya**
1	**clove garlic**
2 to 3	**red chili peppers, seeded**
1	**tomato, sliced in strips**
1 to 2	**tablespoons fish sauce***
3	**tablespoons lime juice**
	Lettuce leaves or cabbage squares
1	**lime, cut into wedges**
Garnish:	**Red chili peppers (optional)**

Peel and seed papaya; shred. Grind together garlic and red chili peppers in a food processor or mortar. Mix together the papaya, tomato, fish sauce and lime juice; add in garlic mixture and toss lightly. Place a portion of papaya mixture onto a lettuce leaf or cabbage square and form into a packet to eat. Serve with wedges of lime. Garnish with red chili peppers. Makes 4 servings.

Note: Shredded carrots or cucumber can be substituted for the green papaya.

Idea: There are many variations of papaya salad in Southeast Asia. Thais like theirs with ground peanuts, sugar and salted shrimp powder. The Laotian version usually calls for pickled fresh water crabs and long string beans. Vietnamese like theirs with beef jerky and mint leaves.

*The amount of fish sauce used in this recipe depends on the brand selected and personal taste.

SEAFOOD, POULTRY AND MEAT

Asparagus with Shrimp and Black Mushrooms — 63
Thai Shrimp with Garlic — 64
Shrimp with Red Chili Paste — 65
Sa-Teh Shrimp — 67
Steamed Fish Eggs with Dill — 68
Thai Sweet and Sour Fish — 69
Whole Fish with Fresh Ginger and Yellow Bean Sauce — 72
Opakapaka with Red Curry Sauce — 73
Crab Legs with Yellow Bean Sauce — 76
Scallops with Fresh Basil — 80
Shrimp with Mixed Vegetables — 81
Fried Mussels with Fresh Whole Chili Peppers — 84
Steamed Clams with Fresh Ginger — 85
Stuffed Crab — 87
Chicken with Fresh Sweet Basil — 88
Bar-B-Que Chicken — 89
Evil Jungle Prince with Chicken — 92
Thai Roast Duck — 93
Eggplant with Chicken — 95
Roast Duck with Chili — 96
Chicken with Black Mushrooms — 97
Cashew Chicken — 99
Beef with String Beans and Fresh Ginger — 100
Beef with Fresh Sweet Basil — 101
Beef with Oyster Sauce — 104
Crispy Fried Beef — 105

Asparagus is very popular among the Chinese-Thai in Bangkok. This combination of asparagus with Chinese black mushrooms is a delicious and a simple dish to prepare. For hot-food lovers, add a few chili peppers.

ASPARAGUS WITH SHRIMP AND BLACK MUSHROOMS

(Illustrated on opposite page)

½	**pound shrimp**
1	**pound fresh asparagus**
1	**ounce dried Chinese black mushrooms**
2	**tablespoons oil**
2	**cloves garlic, minced**
3	**tablespoons oyster sauce**
2 to 4	**red chili peppers, seeded and sliced (optional)**

Method 1: Shell and devein shrimp; set aside. Rinse asparagus; peel and trim stems. Cut into 3-inch lengths. Soak mushrooms in warm water for 15 minutes; drain and discard stems. Slice caps into 1-inch strips. In a skillet heat oil; add garlic and cook until light brown. Stir in mushrooms and cook, stirring constantly, for 1 minute. Add shrimp, asparagus, oyster sauce and red chili peppers; stir fry for 3 minutes. Serve hot. Makes 3 to 4 servings.

Method 2: Shell and devein shrimp set aside. Rinse asparagus; peel and trim stems. Soak mushrooms in warm water for 15 minutes; drain and discard stems. Leave caps whole. Steam shrimp, asparagus and mushrooms for 10 minutes or until the shrimp are cooked. Remove from steamer and arrange on a platter. In a skillet heat oil; add garlic and cook until light brown. Stir in oyster sauce, then pour over shrimp platter. Serve hot. Makes 3 to 4 servings.

Garlic and black pepper give this stir fried dish the spicy goodness that Thais love so well. Asian garlic is slightly smaller and stronger in fragrance than the Western variety.

THAI SHRIMP WITH GARLIC

¼	cup oil
4	cloves garlic, finely chopped
½	pound shrimp, shelled and deveined
¼	cup coconut milk
¼	cup straw or fresh mushrooms
¼	teaspoon ground black pepper
1 to 2	teaspoons fish sauce* or ¼ teaspoon salt
3	cups chopped cabbage
Garnish:	Chinese parsley sprigs

Heat oil in a wok. Add garlic and stir fry until garlic is golden brown. Stir in shrimp, coconut milk, mushrooms, black pepper and fish sauce; cook for about 10 minutes or until shrimp are cooked. Line a platter with chopped cabbage and top with shrimp. Garnish with Chinese parsley. Makes 2 to 3 servings.

*The amount of fish sauce used in this recipe depends on the brand selected and personal taste.

Stir fried shrimp with chili paste and fresh sweet basil leaves are a real classic of Thai home cooking.

SHRIMP WITH RED CHILI PASTE

1	**pound medium fresh shrimp**
6	**tablespoons oil**
1	**teaspoon red chili paste**
1 to 4	**tablespoons fish sauce***
1	**teaspoon brown sugar or honey**
20	**sweet basil leaves**

Shell and devein shrimp, leaving tails on for color. Heat oil in a wok on high heat with chili paste until it starts to bubble. Add shrimp, fish sauce and brown sugar; stir fry for 3 to 5 minutes or until shrimp are cooked. Stir in sweet basil leaves just before serving. Makes 3 to 4 servings.

*The amount of fish sauce used in this recipe depends on the brand selected and personal taste.

An enticing shrimp dish in a superbly seasoned Thai peanut sauce.

SA-TEH SHRIMP

(Illustrated on opposite page)

1	**pound shrimp**
¼	**cup oil**
2	**cloves garlic, minced**
1	**onion, chopped**
½ to 1	**teaspoon ground dried red chili peppers**
3	**kaffir lime leaves**
½	**teaspoon curry powder**
1	**tablespoon chopped fresh lemon grass**
1	**cup coconut milk**
½	**cup milk**
1	**2-inch cinnamon stick**
3	**bay leaves**
2	**teaspoons tamarind sauce**
1 to 3	**tablespoons fish sauce***
3	**tablespoons dark brown sugar**
3	**tablespoons lemon juice**
1	**cup chunky peanut butter**
3	**cups water**
1	**cup chopped cabbage**
1	**tomato, cut into wedges**

Shell and devein shrimp; set aside. Heat oil in a skillet to medium-high heat and saute garlic, onion, red chili peppers, kaffir lime leaves, curry powder and lemon grass for 2 to 3 minutes. Stir in coconut milk, milk, cinnamon stick, bay leaves, tamarind sauce, fish sauce, brown sugar, lemon juice and peanut butter; mix well. Reduce heat and cook, stirring frequently, until sauce thickens, about 30 minutes. Be very careful sauce does not stick to bottom of pan. Bring water to a boil; add shrimp and cook 3 minutes. Place chopped cabbage on serving platter and top with shrimp and tomato wedges. Pour on sauce. Makes 4 servings.

*The amount of fish sauce used in this recipe depends on the brand selected and personal taste.

Young dill leaves are often used in fish dishes in Northern Thailand and Laos. Thais call it "pak chee lao" meaning Laotian parsley. *Eryngium foetidum* is another edible leaf in Laotian cooking and also is commonly used in Vietnam as a garnish for noodle soups. Caution . . . both dill and *eryngium foetidum* have very strong flavors.

STEAMED FISH EGGS WITH DILL

2	cups fish eggs
2	ounces firm white fish fillet
$1/_8$	teaspoon salt
3	dried red chili peppers
6	shallots, chopped
4	cloves garlic, finely chopped
1	ounce fresh dill, cut into 2-inch strips
5	eryngium foetidum leaves, finely chopped
2 to 4	tablespoons fish sauce*
1	teaspoon cornstarch
2	eggs
Garnish:	Fresh dill

Rinse fish eggs in cold water, then set aside. Mince fish filet; add salt and mix well. Remove seeds from dried red chili peppers, then soak in warm water for 5 minutes; drain and finely chop. Combine fish eggs, fish, red chili peppers, shallots, garlic, dill, eryngium foetidum leaves, fish sauce, cornstarch and eggs; blend well. Pour mixture into a 2-inch deep pan and steam for 40 minutes. Serve warm. Garnish with fresh dill. Makes 3 to 4 servings.

Note: Chopped shrimp can be substituted for the fish eggs. A gourmet delight, yet amazingly easy.

*The amount of fish sauce used in this recipe depends on the brand selected and personal taste.

Traditionally, this sweet and sour sauce has more vegetables and less corn-starch than the Chinese variety.

THAI SWEET AND SOUR FISH

2	**pound whole snapper**
4	**cups oil for deep frying**
4	**tablespoons cornstarch**
1	**pound mixed vegetables (refer to page 81)**
3	**cloves garlic, finely chopped**
¼	**cup tomato sauce**
2	**tablespoons red wine vinegar**
1 to 2	**tablespoons fish sauce***
2	**tablespoons sugar**
½	**teaspoon salt**
4 to 6	**red chili peppers, seeded and sliced (optional)**
½	**cup water**
Garnish:	**Chinese parsley sprigs**

Rinse fish well under running cold water. Score fish on both sides on the diagonal in a crosshatch pattern every ¾-inch, cutting half way to the bone. Coat fish lightly with 2 tablespoons of the cornstarch. Cut vegetables into 1 to 2-inch strips. Heat oil in a large wok on high heat until oil begins to get hot. Lower whole fish into the wok and reduce heat to medium. Cook for about 20 to 25 minutes or until fish is cooked and crisp, being careful not to over cook. Set aside on a large platter. Heat 2 tablespoons of the oil and the garlic in a frying pan on medium heat until garlic is golden brown. Stir in mixed vegetables, tomato sauce, red wine vinegar, fish sauce, sugar, salt and red chili peppers. Combine the remaining 2 tablespoons cornstarch and water; blend to make a smooth paste. Stir cornstarch mixture into sauce and cook 5 minutes or until vegetables are cooked and sauce is thickened. Pour over fish and serve hot. Garnish with Chinese parsley.

*The amount of fish sauce used in this recipe depends on the brand selected and personal taste.

Choose any seasonal red snapper, swordfish, tuna or firm white fish. Deep fry in a large wok. Serve with zesty Thai sauce and garnishes. A magnificient show-off entree.

WHOLE FISH WITH FRESH GINGER AND YELLOW BEAN SAUCE

(Illustrated on pages 70 and 71)

2	pound whole fish
1	ounce dried Chinese black mushrooms
2	cloves garlic, chopped
½	cup thinly sliced shallots
2	tablespoons shredded common ginger
2	tablespoons brown sugar
1 to 5	red chili peppers, seeded and chopped (optional)
1	tablespoon yellow bean sauce*
1	tablespoon oyster sauce
3	green onions, cut into 2-inch lengths
1	tablespoon cornstarch
½	cup cold water
6	cups oil for deep frying
3	tablespoons rice flour
3	cups chopped cabbage
Garnish:	Red chili peppers
	Chinese parsley sprigs, cut into 2-inch lengths

Rinse fish well under running cold water. Score fish on both sides on the diagonal in a crosshatch pattern every ¾-inch, cutting half way to the bone. Soak Chinese black mushrooms in warm water for 15 minutes; drain and discard stems. Cut caps into strips. In a saucepan heat 3 tablespoons of the oil. Add mushrooms, garlic and shallots and cook on medium heat, until golden brown. Add ginger, brown sugar, red chili peppers, yellow bean sauce, oyster sauce and green onions; mix well. Dissolve cornstarch in cold water and add to sauce; stir well. Reduce heat and simmer until sauce is thick. Pat fish dry with absorbent paper towels. In a large wok heat remaining oil for deep frying on high heat for about 4 minutes. Coat fish with rice flour. Carefully place fish in oil, then immediately lower heat to medium. Fry fish until golden brown, about 10 to 15 minutes, depending on the thickness of the fish. Drain fish on absorbent paper towels to remove excess oil. Place chopped cabbage on a large platter and top with fish and pour on sauce. Garnish with red chili peppers and Chinese parsley. Makes 4 to 6 servings.

*Yellow bean sauce from Thailand is saltier than sauce from Hong Kong or China. Season to taste.

Any firm white fish substitutes well in this recipe for crisp fried whole fish. Thai gourmets like it extra crispy. Catfish or mudfish are the favorites selected by Thai chefs for this dish.

OPAKAPAKA WITH RED CURRY SAUCE

2	**pound whole opakapaka (or any firm white fish)**
2	**tablespoons cornstarch**
	Oil for deep frying
½	**small head cabbage, chopped**
¼	**cup oil**
3	**tablespoons Red Curry Sauce (recipe page 126)**
1	**cup coconut milk**
2 to 4	**tablespoons fish sauce***
10 to 15	**sweet basil leaves**

Clean fish. Score fish on both sides on the diagonal in a crosshatch pattern every ¾-inch, cutting half way to the bone. Coat fish lightly with the cornstarch. Heat oil for deep frying to 350F. Fry fish for 15 to 20 minutes or until fish is cooked and crisp, being careful not to overcook. Line a serving platter with chopped cabbage and place fish on top. Set aside. Heat the ¼ cup oil on medium-high heat and saute Red Curry Sauce for 3 minutes. Stir in coconut milk and cook for 2 minutes. Reduce heat to medium-low; stir in fish sauce and basil. Cook for 3 minutes. Pour over fish. Makes 3 to 4 servings.

*The amount of fish sauce used in this recipe depends on the brand selected and personal taste.

Almost all seafood restaurants in Thailand serve a version of this crab leg with yellow bean sauce and green. A mild but colorful dish.

CRAB LEGS WITH YELLOW BEAN SAUCE

(Illustrated on pages 74 and 75)

2	pounds crab legs
1	teaspoon cornstarch
¼	cup cold water
¼	cup oil
2	cloves garlic, chopped
½	onion, thinly sliced
1	egg, lightly beaten
1	tablespoon yellow bean sauce*
1	tablespoon oyster sauce
3	green onions, cut into 2-inch lengths
Garnish:	Green onion brushes (directions page 183)

Rinse crab legs and cut into 2 to 3-inch lengths; crack shells. Combine cornstarch and cold water; stir to dissolve. In a wok heat oil, garlic and onion on high heat until garlic browns. Stir in egg; mix well. Add crab, yellow bean sauce, oyster sauce and cornstarch mixture. Reduce heat to medium and cook for 10 to 15 minutes or until crab is cooked. Be careful not to overcook crab. Stir in green onions. Garnish with green onion brush. Serve hot. Makes 4 servings.

*Yellow bean sauce from Thailand is saltier than sauce from Hong Kong or China. Season to taste.

In Thailand lobster tails are usually not served whole, but rather cut into bite size pieces before cooking. This is a very unusual dish, but delicious!

LOBSTER WITH PINEAPPLE

4	**lobster tails (6 ounces each)**
¼	**cup oil**
3	**cloves garlic, chopped**
1	**stalk fresh lemon grass, finely chopped**
1	**teaspoon Red Curry Paste (recipe page 126)**
1	**egg, lightly beaten**
½	**cup water**
1	**cup pineapple chunks**
2 to 4	**tablespoons fish sauce***
½	**teaspoon brown sugar**
15 to 20	**sweet basil leaves**

Slit underside of lobster and press lightly to open. In a skillet heat oil on high heat; add garlic, lemon grass and red curry paste and cook until sauce bubbles. Stir in egg and cook for 1 minute. Add lobster and water and bring to a boil. Reduce heat to medium and add pineapple, fish sauce and brown sugar. Cook for 5 to 10 minutes or until lobster is cooked, but not overcooked. Stir in sweet basil. Serve immediately. Makes 4 servings.

*The amount of fish sauce used in this recipe depends on the brand used and personal taste.

Fresh basil is excellent for stir frying with seafood or poultry. Add a touch of garlic.

SCALLOPS WITH FRESH BASIL

(Illustrated on pages 78 and 79)

½	**pound fresh scallops**
2	**tablespoons oil**
3	**cloves garlic, peeled, chopped**
3	**kaffir lime leaves, cut in thin strips**
½	**cup mushrooms (preferably straw mushrooms)**
¼	**cup shredded bamboo shoots**
3	**tablespoons oyster sauce**
2 to 4	**red chili peppers, seeded and chopped (optional)**
15	**sweet basil leaves**
2	**cups chopped cabbage (optional)**

Rinse scallops and score diagonally. In a wok heat oil, garlic and kaffir lime leaves on high heat, until oil bubbles. Add scallops, mushrooms, bamboo shoots, oyster sauce and red chili peppers; stir fry for 5 minutes or until scallops are cooked. Mix in basil and serve on a bed of chopped cabbage. Makes 2 to 4 servings.

Note: The picture of this recipe is highly stylized. The version that you prepare will probably be more blended.

Shrimp with mixed vegetables is very easy to prepare and takes only minutes to cook. Serve immediately after cooking for the freshest taste and appearance.

SHRIMP WITH MIXED VEGETABLES

½	**pound bay shrimp**
2	**tablespoons oil**
2	**cloves garlic, minced**
½	**pound mixed vegetables***
3 to 4	**tablespoons oyster sauce**

Rinse shrimp and pat dry. In a skillet heat oil; add garlic and cook until light brown. Stir in shrimp and cook 1 to 2 minutes, stirring constantly. Stir in mixed vegetables and oyster sauce and cook for 3 minutes. Makes 4 servings.

*Select from the following vegetables:
  bell peppers
  string beans
  water chestnuts
  tomatoes
  bamboo shoots
  miniature corn
  asparagus
  cucumbers
  zucchini
  mushrooms

Thai beaches are full of eateries and sidewalk food peddlers. Fried mussels are one of the favorite dishes for beachgoers.

FRIED MUSSELS WITH FRESH WHOLE CHILI PEPPERS

(Illustrated on page 82)

½	**pound mussels without shells**
¼	**cup oil**
4	**cloves garlic, finely chopped**
4	**shallots, finely chopped**
1 to 3	**teaspoons yellow bean sauce***
10 to 20	**small red chili peppers**
1	**tablespoon cornstarch**
¼	**cup cold water**
Garnish:	**Chinese parsley sprigs, cut into 2-inch lengths**

Rinse mussels and pat dry on paper towels. Heat oil on high heat in a wok with garlic and shallots until golden brown. Add mussels, yellow bean sauce and red chili peppers; stir fry for 7 to 10 minutes. Dissolve cornstarrch in cold water and stir into sauce in wok. Stir until sauce thickens. Garnish with Chinese parsley. Makes 2 to 4 servings.

*Yellow bean sauce from Thailand is saltier than sauce from Hong Kong or China. Season to taste.

Seafood is abundant in Thailand especially at all the beach resorts. This combination of clams with fresh ginger is delicious and simple.

STEAMED CLAMS WITH FRESH GINGER

(Illustrated on page 83)

2	pounds fresh clams
2	cloves garlic, chopped
½	onion, thinly sliced
3	green onions, cut into 2-inch lengths
2	tablespoons thinly slivered ginger
1 to 2	tablespoons yellow bean sauce*
1	tablespoon oyster sauce
1 to 2	red chili peppers, seeded and cut into thin strips (optional)

Rinse clams. Combine all the remaining ingredients. Pour sauce over clams and mix well. Steam for 15 minutes or until clams open up. Serve hot. Makes 4 servings.

*Yellow bean sauce from Thailand is saltier than sauce from Hong Kong or China. Season to taste.

Sensational seafood dish. Everybodys favorite. Stuffed crab shells with fresh crabmeat, shrimp, mushrooms, long rice and other vegetables.

STUFFED CRAB

(Illustrated on opposite page)

5	**large crabs**
4	**ounces dried Chinese black mushrooms**
2	**ounces bean threads**
6	**ounces shrimp, shelled and deveined**
1	**onion, chopped**
1	**carrot, shredded**
6	**water chestnuts, chopped**
1	**egg**
½	**teaspoon cornstarch**
2	**teaspoons fish sauce or ½ teaspoon salt**
¼	**teaspoon ground black pepper**
	Oil for deep frying
Garnish:	**Spring Roll Sauce (recipe page 120)**
	Green onions
	Red chili flowers (directions page 179)

Steam whole crabs for about 30 minutes or until cooked. Remove crabmeat from shells and set shells aside. Soak Chinese black mushrooms and bean threads in warm water in seperate containers for 15 minutes. Drain Chinese black mushrooms; discard stems and finely chop. Drain bean threads and cut into 1-inch lengths. Finely chop crabmeat and shrimp. Combine crabmeat, shrimp, Chinese black mushrooms, bean threads, onion, carrot, water chestnuts, egg, cornstarch, fish sauce and pepper; blend well. Stuff shells with crabmeat mixture. Heat oil for deep frying to medium heat. Deep fry shells for 12 to 15 minutes or until golden brown. Drain on absorbent paper towels. Serve with Spring Roll Sauce. Garnish with green onions and red chili flowers. Makes 5 servings.

The original Thai dish with basil, garlic, and chili peppers is an excellent introduction to Thai cuisine. Most Thais prefer hot basil which has a much stronger taste than the milder sweet basil.

CHICKEN WITH FRESH SWEET BASIL

½	**pound boneless chicken breast**
2	**tablespoons oil**
3	**cloves garlic, chopped**
3	**kaffir lime leaves, cut in thin strips**
½	**cup mushrooms (preferably straw mushrooms)**
¼	**cup shredded bamboo shoots**
3	**tablespoons oyster sauce**
2 to 4	**red chili peppers, seeded and chopped (optional)**
15	**sweet basil leaves**
2	**cups chopped cabbage (optional)**

Thinly cut beef into 2-inch strips. In a wok heat oil, garlic and kaffir lime leaves on high heat, until oil bubbles. Add chicken, mushrooms, bamboo shoots, oyster sauce and red chili peppers; stir fry for 5 minutes or until chicken is cooked. Mix in basil and serve on a bed of chopped cabbage. Makes 2 to 4 servings.

Barbecued chicken is so popular in Thailand it is served almost every-where . . . from portable food stations, bus stops, stadiums, to beaches.

BAR-B-QUE CHICKEN

2	whole young chickens
4	stalks fresh lemon grass
1	tablespoon coarsely chopped fresh ginger
1	ounce garlic, finely chopped (about 6 large cloves)
4	shallots
½	cup coarsely chopped Chinese parsley roots
3	tablespoons brown sugar
½	cup coconut milk
1 to 2	tablespoons fish sauce*
2	tablespoons soy sauce
2	tablespoons oil
	Hot sticky rice (recipe page 148)
Garnish:	Chinese parsley sprigs, cut into 2-inch lengths
	Red chili peppers (optional)

Rinse chickens and pat dry. Split chickens down the breast, but do not cut all the way through; press open. Place chickens in a large bowl. In a food processor or blender combine lemon grass, ginger, garlic, shal-lots, parsley roots, brown sugar, coconut milk, fish sauce, soy sauce and oil; blend until smooth. Pour sauce over chickens and marinate over-night in the refrigerator. Preheat oven to 350F. Place chickens on a rack in an open pan with the split side down. Bake for about one hour, depend-ing on the thickness of the chicken, or until the juices run clear when the thigh is pierced with a sharp knife. Serve with hot sticky rice. Gar-nish with Chinese parsley and red chili peppers. Makes 4 to 6 servings.

*The amount of fish sauce used in this recipe depends on the brand selected and personal taste.

This spicy-flavored dish has quite a reputation for its unique name (developed by Keo himself in 1977 for his Mekong restaurant), and has been mentioned in such publications as BON APPETIT, FOOD AND WINE, BAZAAR, and the NEW YORK and LOS ANGELES TIMES. Fresh basil, coconut milk, and red chili form a flavor for the gourmet's delight.

EVIL JUNGLE PRINCE WITH CHICKEN

(Illustrated on pages 90 and 91)

½	**pound boneless chicken breast**
2 to 6	**small red chili peppers**
½	**stalk fresh lemon grass**
2	**kaffir lime leaves**
2	**tablespoons oil**
½	**cup coconut milk**
½	**teaspoon salt**
1 to 4	**tablespoons fish sauce***
10 to 15	**sweet basil leaves**
1	**cup chopped cabbage**

Thinly cut chicken into 2-inch strips. Grind together red chili peppers, lemon grass and kaffir lime leaves in a food processor or pound in a mortar. Heat oil to medium-high and saute pepper mixture for 3 minutes. Stir in coconut milk and cook for 2 minutes. Add chicken and cook for 5 minutes or until cooked. Reduce heat to medium-low. Stir in fish sauce and basil. Serve on bed of chopped cabbage. Makes 3 to 4 servings.

*The amount of fish sauce used in this recipe depends on the brand selected and personal taste.

Duck is not used as much in Thai cooking as in Chinese.

THAI ROAST DUCK

1	**duck, about 3 pounds**
2 to 4	**red chili peppers, seeded and finely chopped**
1	**teaspoon Chinese five spice powder**
1	**tablespoon brown sugar**
1	**teaspoon honey**
1	**teaspoon lemon juice**
½	**teaspoon salt**
½	**teaspoon grated common ginger**
1	**teaspoon soy sauce**
1	**teaspoon sesame oil**
2	**cloves garlic**

Rinse duck and pat dry. Combine all the remaining ingredients in a food processor or blender; blend until smooth. Rub mixture all over and inside the duck. Preheat oven to 375F. Place a wire rack in a shallow roasting pan; add a little water to the pan to reduce spattering of fat during cooking. Place duck on the rack. Bake for 1 hour or until duck is cooked. Makes 4 to 6 servings.

A gourmet delight, yet amazingly easy.

EGGPLANT WITH CHICKEN

(Illustrated on opposite page)

¾	**pound Japanese eggplant (about 3 cups sliced)**
⅓	**pound boneless chicken breast**
6	**tablespoons oil**
2 to 3	**cloves garlic, crushed**
1 to 5	**red chili peppers, seeded and chopped**
10 to 15	**sweet basil leaves**
1 to 3	**tablespoons yellow bean sauce***

Slice unpeeled eggplant crosswise into slices $1/8$-inch thick. Thinly slice chicken. Heat oil in a wok; add garlic and stir fry until light brown. Add eggplant and chicken and cook for 5 to 7 minutes. Add red chili peppers, basil leaves and yellow bean sauce; mix well. Serve immediately, since eggplant and basil turn dark if dish sits after cooking. Makes 3 to 4 servings.

*Yellow bean sauce from Thailand is saltier than sauce from Hong Kong or China. Season to taste.

Roast duck pieces stir fried with red dried chili peppers, garlic and shallots makes a very spicy and delicious dish. This is a favorite among the "Chinese Thais" in Bangkok.

ROAST DUCK WITH CHILI

1	**roast duck**
¼	**cup oil**
8	**cloves garlic, chopped**
10	**shallots, chopped**
1	**stalk fresh lemon grass, finely chopped**
1	**ounce Chinese parsley roots, chopped**
1	**teaspoon cornstarch**
¼	**cup cold water**
20 to 30	**large dried red chili peppers, soaked, drained and seeded**
2 to 4	**tablespoons fish sauce***
1	**teaspoon soy sauce**
1	**teaspoon cornstarch**
¼	**cup cold water**
2 to 3	**tablespoons brown sugar or honey**
Garnish:	**Chinese parsley sprigs**

Cut duck into serving pieces. In a skillet heat oil; add garlic, shallots, lemon grass and Chinese parsley roots and cook until light brown. Combine cornstarch and water; blend to make a smooth paste. Stir duck, red chili peppers, fish sauce, soy sauce, cornstarch mixture and brown sugar into duck. Reduce heat to medium and cook for 10 minutes. Garnish with Chinese parsley. Serve with hot steamed rice. makes 4 to 6 servings.

*The amount of fish sauce used in this recipe depends on the brand selected and personal taste.

Many people believe this dish originated in China. Chinese influence in Thai and other Southeast Asian cuisine is undeniable, however, they all have developed their own nuances.

CHICKEN WITH BLACK MUSHROOMS

1	**pound boneless chicken breast**
10	**large dried Chinese black mushrooms**
¼	**cup oil**
3	**cloves garlic, chopped**
4	**shallots, chopped**
½	**ounce common ginger, shredded**
1	**teaspoon cornstarch**
¼	**cup water**
2 to 4	**tablespoons fish sauce***
2	**tablespoons brown sugar or honey**
¼	**teaspoon salt**
Garnish:	**Chinese parsley sprigs**
	1 green onion, cut into 2-inch lengths
	3 red chili peppers, seeded and thinly sliced

Thinly cut chicken into 2-inch strips. Soak Chinese black mushrooms in warm water for 15 minutes; drain and discard stems. Slice mushrooms into 1-inch strips. In a skillet heat oil; add garlic, shallots and ginger and cook until light brown. Add chicken. Combine cornstarch and water; blend to make a smooth paste. Stir mushrooms, cornstarch mixture, fish sauce, brown sugar and salt into chicken. Stir fry for 2 minutes, then reduce heat to medium and cook for 10 minutes or until chicken is cooked. Garnish with Chinese parsley, green onion and red chili peppers. Serve with hot steamed rice. Makes 2 to 3 servings.

*The amount of fish sauce used in this recipe depends on the brand selected and personal taste.

An easy, exotic dish of roasted cashew nuts stir fried with tender slices of chicken, green onions, oyster sauce and a touch of garlic.

CASHEW CHICKEN

(Illustrated on opposite page)

¾	pound boneless chicken breast
¼	cup oil
2	cloves garlic, crushed
2	tablespoons oyster sauce
8	green onions, cut into 2-inch lengths
1 to 5	whole dried red chili peppers
¾	pound unsalted roasted cashew nuts (about 3 cups)
4	large lettuce leaves
Garnish:	Green onion brush (directions page 183)

Thinly slice chicken. Heat oil in a wok; add garlic and stir fry until light brown. Add chicken and oyster sauce and cook for 4 to 6 minutes. Reduce heat to medium. Add green onions, red chili peppers and cashew nuts; mix well. Place lettuce leaves on a platter and top with chicken. Garnish with green onion brush. Makes 3 to 4 servings.

This spicy hot dish is made with all fresh ingredients. A delightfully different recipe.

BEEF WITH STRING BEANS AND FRESH GINGER

½   **pound beef**
½   **pound fresh string beans**
2   **tablespoons oil**
1   **stalk fresh lemon grass, finely chopped**
1   **tablespoon shredded common ginger**
1 to 5   **red chili peppers, seeded and finely chopped**
½   **cup coconut milk**
¼   **teaspoon salt**
3   **cups chopped cabbage (optional)**

Thinly slice beef into 2-inch strips. Cut string beans into 2-inch strips.
Heat oil in a wok with lemon grass, ginger and red chili peppers on high
heat, until oil bubbles. Add beef, coconut milk, string beans and salt;
stir fry for 3 minutes or until beef is cooked. Served on a bed of chopped
cabbage. Makes 6 servings.

Stirfry beef with fresh sweet basil accompanied, of course, by steamed rice is to a Thai as meat and potatoes are to an American.

BEEF WITH FRESH SWEET BASIL

½	**pound beef**
2	**tablespoons oil**
3	**cloves garlic, chopped**
3	**kaffir lime leaves, cut in thin strips**
½	**cup mushrooms (preferably straw mushrooms)**
¼	**cup shredded bamboo shoots**
3	**tablespoons oyster sauce**
2 to 4	**red chili peppers, seeded and chopped (optional)**
15	**sweet basil leaves**
2	**cups chopped cabbage (optional)**

Thinly cut beef into 2-inch strips. Heat oil in a wok with garlic and kaffir lime leaves on high heat, until oil bubbles. Add beef, mushrooms, bamboo shoots, oyster sauce and red chili peppers; stir fry for 5 minutes or until beef is cooked. Mix in basil and serve on a bed of chopped cabbage. Makes 2 to 4 servings.

This is a good recipe when you don't know exactly how many to expect for dinner. Just make extra. It's good the next day.

BEEF WITH OYSTER SAUCE

(Illustrated on pages 102 and 103)

1   **pound flank steak**
1   **ounce dried Chinese black mushrooms**
2   **tablespoons oil**
2   **cloves garlic, minced**
3   **tablespoons oyster sauce**

Thinly slice flank steak on the diagonal into strips 1-inch wide by 2 to 3-inches in length. Soak Chinese black mushrooms in warm water for 15 minutes; drain and discard stems. Thinly slice mushroom caps. In a skillet heat oil; add garlic and cook until light brown. Stir in beef and cook 1 to 2 minutes, stirring constantly. Stir in mushrooms and cook for 1 minute. Add oyster sauce and cook for 1 minute. Makes 4 servings.

Sometimes also called Dried Salted Beef, these marinated strips of flank steak are popular served with a salad and sticky rice. Thai men favor them as hors d'oeuvres with cold beer.

CRISPY FRIED BEEF

3	**pounds flank steak**
3	**stalks fresh lemon grass, finely chopped**
1	**ounce garlic, peeled and finely chopped (about 6 large cloves)**
1 to 4	**tablespoons fish sauce* or 2 teaspoons salt**
2	**teaspoons brown sugar**
½	**teaspoon ground black pepper**
2	**tablespoons oil**
3	**tablespoons rice flour**
3	**tablespoons chopped Chinese parsley roots**
3	**cups oil for deep frying** **Spring Roll Sauce (recipe page 120)**
Garnish:	**Chinese parsley sprigs**

Slice beef into thin strips about 3 to 4-inches in length. In a bowl combine beef, lemon grass, garlic, fish sauce, brown sugar, black pepper, oil, rice flour and Chinese parsley roots; mix well. Marinate beef in the refrigerator overnight. In a wok heat the oil for deep frying on medium heat until oil is hot. Place the meat, piece by piece, in the oil and fry until the meat is dry and cooked, about 15 minutes. Remove meat; drain thoroughly on absorbent paper towels. Let cool before serving. Serve at room temperature with Spring Roll Sauce, if desired. Garnish with Chinese parsley sprigs. Makes 6 to 8 servings.

*The amount of fish sauce used in this recipe depends on the brand selected and personal taste.

VEGETABLE DISHES

String Beans with Fresh Ginger — 109
Eggplant with Tofu — 110
Stir Fried Ong Choi with Yellow Bean Sauce — 111
Evil Jungle Prince with Mixed Vegetables — 113
Thai Sweet and Sour Vegetables — 114
Asparagus with Black Mushrooms — 115

This spicy hot vegetarian dish is made with all fresh ingredients. A delightfully different recipe.

STRING BEANS WITH FRESH GINGER

(Illustrated on opposite page)

½   **pound fresh string beans**
2   **tablespoons oil**
1   **stalk fresh lemon grass, finely chopped**
1   **tablespoon shredded common ginger**
1 to 5   **red chili peppers, seeded and finely chopped**
½   **cup coconut milk**
¼   **teaspoon salt**
3   **cups chopped cabbage**

Cut string beans into 2-inch strips. Heat oil in a wok with lemon grass, ginger and red chili peppers until oil starts to bubble. Stir in coconut milk, string beans and salt; cook on high heat for 3 minutes. Serve on a bed of chopped cabbage. Makes 6 servings.

A gourmet delight, yet amazingly easy.

EGGPLANT WITH TOFU

¾	**pound Japanese eggplant (about 3 cups sliced)**
¼	**pound tofu**
6	**tablespoons oil**
2 to 3	**cloves garlic, crushed**
1 to 5	**red chili peppers, seeded and chopped**
10 to 15	**sweet basil leaves**
1 to 3	**tablespoons yellow bean sauce***

Slice unpeeled egglplant crosswise into slices $1/_8$-inch thick. Cut tofu into ½-inch cubes. Heat oil in skillet; add garlic and stir fry until light brown. Add eggplant and tofu and cook for 5 to 7 minutes. Add remaining ingredients; mix gently. Serve immediately, since eggplant and basil turn dark if dish sits after cooking. Makes 3 to 4 servings.

*Yellow bean sauce from Thailand is saltier than sauce from Hong Kong or China. Season to taste.

Ong choi (Asian watercress) stir fried with bean sauce or fish sauce is very popular in Thailand.

STIR FRIED ONG CHOI WITH YELLOW BEAN SAUCE

¼	cup oil
3	cloves garlic, finely chopped
2	pounds ong choi, cut into 2-inch lengths
1 to 3	teaspoons yellow bean sauce*
2	teaspoons oyster sauce or ¹/₈ teaspoon salt
3 to 5	red chili peppers, seeded and thinly sliced (optional)

Heat oil on high heat in a large wok with garlic until golden brown. Add ong choi, yellow bean sauce, oyster sauce and red chili peppers; stir fry for 2 minutes or until the ong choi softens. Serve immediately, since ong choi darkens a few minutes after it is cooked.

Note: Broccoli, head cabbage, spinach or cauliflower can be substituted for the ong choi.

*Yellow bean sauce from Thailand is saltier than sauce from Hong Kong or China. Season to taste.

The most popular vegetarian dish at all of Keo's restaurants.

EVIL JUNGLE PRINCE WITH MIXED VEGETABLES

(Illustrated on opposite page)

½	**pound mixed vegetables (refer to page 81)**
6	**small red chili peppers**
½	**stalk fresh lemon grass**
2	**kaffir lime leaves**
2	**tablespoons oil**
½	**cup coconut milk**
¼	**teaspoon of salt**
10 to 15	**sweet basil leaves**
1	**cup chopped cabbage**

Cut vegetables into thin strips. Grind together red chili peppers, lemon grass and kaffir lime leaves in a food processor or pound in a mortar. Heat oil to medium-high and saute pepper mixture for 3 minutes. Stir in coconut milk and cook for 2 minutes. Add vegetables and cook for 5 minutes. Reduce heat to medium-low. Stir in salt and basil. Serve on bed of chopped cabbage. Makes 3 to 4 servings.

"More vegetables! Less cornstarch!" That's what makes this Thai sweet and sour dish so extra good and somewhat different than the Chinese.

THAI SWEET AND SOUR VEGETABLES

1	**pound mixed vegetables (refer to page 81)**
2	**tablespoons oil**
3	**cloves garlic, finely chopped**
¼	**cup tomato sauce**
2	**tablespoons red wine vinegar**
1 to 2	**tablespoons fish sauce***
2	**tablespoons sugar**
½	**teaspoon salt**
4 to 6	**red chili peppers, seeded and sliced (optional)**
2	**tablespoons cornstarch**
½	**cup water**

Cut vegetables into 1 to 2-inch strips. Heat oil and the garlic in a frying pan on medium heat until garlic is golden brown. Stir in mixed vegetables, tomato sauce, red wine vinegar, fish sauce, sugar, salt and red chili peppers. Combine the cornstarch and water; blend to make a smooth paste. Stir cornstarch mixture into sauce and cook 5 minutes or until vegetables are cooked and sauce is thickened. Makes 3 to 4 servings.

*The amount of fish sauce used in this recipe depends on the brand selected and personal taste.

Asparagus is very popular among the Chinese-Thai in Bangkok. This combination of asparagus with Chinese black mushrooms is really delicious and a very simple dish to prepare. Hot-food lovers, add a few chili peppers.

ASPARAGUS WITH BLACK MUSHROOMS

1	pound fresh or canned asparagus
1	ounce dried Chinese black mushrooms
2	tablespoons oil
2	cloves garlic, minced
3 to 4	tablespoons oyster sauce
2 to 4	red chili peppers, seeded and sliced (optional)

Rinse asparagus; peel and trim stems. Soak Chinese black mushrooms in warm water for 15 minutes; drain and discard stems. Leave whole or slice into 1-inch strips. In a skillet heat oil; add garlic and cook until light brown. Stir in mushrooms and cook, stirring constantly, for 1 minute. Add asparagus, oyster sauce and red chili peppers; stir fry for 3 minutes. Serve hot. Makes 3 to 4 servings.

SAUCES AND PASTES

Sa-teh Sauce – 119
Spring Roll Sauce – 120
Cucumber Sauce – 121
Regular (Musamun) Curry Paste – 124
Yellow Curry Paste – 125
Red Curry Paste – 126
Green Curry Paste – 127
Thai Curry Sauce – 127

Sa-teh is an excellent dip for assorted chilled vegetables and meats.

SA-TEH SAUCE

(Illustrated on page 118)

¼	**cup oil**
2	**cloves garlic, minced**
1	**onion, chopped**
½ to 1	**teaspoon ground dried red chili peppers**
3	**kaffir lime leaves**
½	**teaspoon curry powder**
1	**tablespoon chopped fresh lemon grass**
1	**cup coconut milk**
½	**cup milk**
1	**2-inch cinnamon stick**
3	**bay leaves**
2	**teaspoons tamarind paste**
1 to 3	**tablespoons fish sauce***
3	**tablespoons dark brown sugar**
3	**tablespoons lemon juice**
1	**cup chunky peanut butter**

Heat oil in a skillet to medium-high heat and saute garlic, onion, chili peppers, kaffir lime leaves, curry powder and lemon grass for 2 to 3 minutes. Stir in coconut milk, milk, cinnamon stick, bay leaves, tamarind sauce, fish sauce, brown sugar, lemon juice and peanut butter; mix well. Reduce heat and cook, stirring frequently, until sauce thickens, about 30 minutes. Be very careful sauce does not stick to bottom of pan.

*The amount of fish sauce used in this recipe depends on the brand selected and personal taste.

Clockwise from top: Sa-teh Sauce (page 119), Cucumber Sauce (page 121), and Spring Roll Sauce (page 120)

Spring Roll sauce can be used as a sauce for almost any deep fried meat or vegetable dish.

SPRING ROLL SAUCE

(Illustrated on page 118)

¼	cup sugar
½	cup water
½	cup red wine vinegar
1 to 2	tablespoons fish sauce* or ½ to 1 teaspoon salt
2 to 3	teaspoons ground red chili peppers
½	carrot or daikon, shredded
¼	cup coarsely chopped peanuts or macadamia nuts

In a small saucepan combine sugar and water; bring to a boil. Reduce heat and simmer for about 10 minutes or until sugar is dissolved. Remove from heat. Stir in red wine vinegar, fish sauce and red chili peppers. Pour sauce into serving bowl. Chill, then top with carrots and sprinkle with peanuts before serving. Makes 1 cup.

*The amount of fish sauce used in this recipe depends on the brand selected and personal taste.

Cucumber Sauce often accompanies Sa-teh dishes and fish patties.

CUCUMBER SAUCE

(Illustrated on page 118)

1	cucumber (preferably Japanese)
5	tablespoons sugar
1	cup boiling water
½	cup white vinegar
1	teaspoon salt
3 to 5	red chili peppers, seeded and finely chopped
3	shallots, finely chopped
Garnish:	6 to 8 sprigs Chinese parsley

Thinly slice cucumber; arrange in a bowl. Dissolve sugar in boiling water; stir in white vinegar and salt. Pour sauce over cucumber slices. Sprinkle with red chili peppers and shallots. Chill. Garnish with Chinese parsley. Makes 1½ cups.

Thai curry pastes are unique because they are always made with fresh leaves, roots and herbs. Whereas Indian curries depend upon dry ingredients.This is a Thai version of a Moslem curry,rich in spices but quite mild and a little sweet.

REGULAR (MUSAMUN) CURRY PASTE

(Illustrated on page 122)

20 to 30	large dried chili peppers, seeded
1	stalk fresh lemon grass, coarsely chopped
1	cup thinly sliced shallots
5	cloves garlic
1	tablespoon coarsely chopped kra chai
10	fresh kaffir lime leaves, chopped
1	tablespoon Chinese parsley root
1	tablespoon Chinese parsley seeds or coriander seeds
1	teaspoon cumin seeds
1	teaspoon salt
½	teaspoon ground cinnamon
1	teaspoon brown sugar
¼	teaspoon shrimp paste (optional)
2	tablespoons oil

Soak dried red chili peppers in water for 5 minutes; drain. Combine all the ingredients in a 2-inch deep pan and bake at 350F. for 15 to 20 minutes. Then process in a food processor until smooth. If a mortar and pestle are used, then add oil after all other ingredients are ground. Refrigerate in a glass container. Paste keeps well for several months.

Top row from left: Regular (Musamun) Curry Sauce, Yellow Curry Sauce, Red Curry Sauce, and Green Curry Sauce

Bottom row from left: Regular (Musamun) Curry Paste (page 124), Yellow Curry Paste (page 125), Red Curry Paste (page 126), and Green Curry Paste (page 127)

Yellow curry is Americans' favorite in Thailand. It is the mildest of all the curries.

YELLOW CURRY PASTE

(Illustrated on page 122)

5 to 10	fresh yellow chili peppers, seeded
1	stalk fresh lemon grass, coarsely chopped
¼	cup thinly sliced shallots
2	tablespoons coarsely chopped garlic
1	teaspoon coarsely chopped kra-chai
1	teaspoon coriander seeds
1	teaspoon caraway seeds
1	teaspoon curry powder
1	teaspoon dried mustard
1	teaspoon salt
½	teaspoon ground cinnamon
1	tablespoon sugar
2	tablespoons oil

Combine all the ingredients in a food processor and process until smooth. If a mortar and pestle is used, then add oil after all other ingredients are ground. Refrigerate in a glass container. Paste keeps well for several months.

The original Thai curry.

RED CURRY PASTE

(Illustrated on pages 122 and 123)

15 to 20 **red chili peppers, seeded**
2 **stalks fresh lemon grass, coarsely chopped**
5 **shallots, thinly sliced**
1 **clove garlic**
1 **tablespoon coarsely chopped kha**
3 **kaffir lime leaves, chopped**
¼ **cup Chinese parsley roots**
½ **teaspoon ground coriander**
½ **teaspoon ground caraway seeds**
½ to 1 **tablespoon fish sauce* or 1 teaspoon salt**
¼ **teaspoon shrimp paste (optional)**
2 **tablespoons oil**

Combine all the ingredients in a food processor and process until smooth. If a mortar and pestle is used, then add oil after all other ingredients are ground. Refrigerate in a glass container. Paste keeps well for several months.

*The amount of fish sauce used in this recipe depends on the brand selected and personal taste.

Another original Thai creation . . . the hottest among all Thai curries.

GREEN CURRY PASTE

(Illustrated on page 123)

15 to 20	fresh small Thai green chili peppers
4	stalks fresh lemon grass, coarsely chopped
3	shallots, thinly sliced
1	clove garlic
1	tablespoon coarsely chopped kha
1	tablespoon coarsely chopped kra-chai
5	kaffir lime leaves, chopped
½	teaspoon chopped kaffir lime rind
½	teaspoon ground coriander
½	teaspoon ground caraway seeds
½ to 1	tablespoon fish sauce* or 1 teaspoon salt
1	tablespoon sugar
¼	teaspoon shrimp paste (optional)
2	tablespoons oil

Combine all the ingredients in a food processor and process until smooth. If a mortar and pestle is used, then add oil after all other ingredients are ground. Refrigerate in a glass container. Paste keeps well for several months.

*The amount of fish sauce used in this recipe depends on the brand selected and personal taste.

Thai curry sauces are made by adding coconut milk to the curry paste. Remember! Amount of paste determines how hot and spicy your sauce will be.

THAI CURRY SAUCE

¼	cup oil
1	teaspoon red, green, yellow or regular curry paste
2	cups coconut milk

Heat oil in a saucepan on high heat. Add curry paste of your choice and stir fry for 1 to 2 minutes; add coconut milk. Bring mixture to a boil, then remove from heat immediately.

CURRIES

Musamun Beef Curry — 131
Yellow Chicken Curry — 132
Thai Crab Curry — 133
Red Pork Curry — 135
Green Shrimp Curry — 136
Panang Duck Curry — 137

Beef chunks sauteed in Thai curry with potatoes and coconut milk, then cooked at low heat to perfection. A favorite of Americans in Thailand.

MUSAMUN BEEF CURRY

(Illustrated on opposite page)

½	**pound beef**
2	**tablespoons oil**
1	**teaspoon Regular (Musamun) Curry Paste (recipe page 124)**
1	**potato, cut into 1-inch cubes**
1	**onion, quartered**
1	**cup coconut milk**
1 to 2	**tablespoons fish sauce***
1	**teaspoon brown sugar**
1 to 5	**red chili peppers, chopped (optional)**
½	**cup roasted peanuts**
	Hot steamed rice

Cut beef into 1-inch cubes. In a saucepan heat oil and regular curry paste on high heat, until curry paste bubbles. Add beef, potato, onion, coconut milk, fish sauce, brown sugar and red chili peppers; stir well and cook for about 10 minutes. Reduce heat and simmer for 30 minutes. Serve immediately. Sprinkle with roasted peanuts. Accompany with hot steamed rice. Makes 4 servings.

Note: Lamb can be substituted for the beef.

*The amount of fish sauce used in this recipe depends on the brand selected and personal taste.

Top: Musamun Beef Curry (page 131)
Bottom: Yellow Chicken Curry (page 132)

Yellow curry is the mildest of all Thai curries. Goes best with chicken or seafood.

YELLOW CHICKEN CURRY

(Illustrated on page 130)

½ **pound boneless chicken breast**
2 **potatoes, peeled**
2 **tablespoons oil**
1 **teaspoon Yellow Curry Paste (recipe page 125)**
1 **cup coconut milk**
2 **tablespoons fish sauce**
1 **teaspoon brown sugar**
1 to 5 **yellow chili peppers, seeded and chopped (optional)**
Hot steamed rice

Thinly slice chicken into 2-inch strips. Cut potatoes into 1-inch cubes. In a saucepan heat oil and yellow curry paste on high heat, until curry paste bubbles. Add chicken, potatoes, coconut milk, fish sauce, brown sugar and yellow chili peppers; stir well and cook for about 7 minutes or until chicken is cooked. Serve immediately. Accompany with hot steamed rice. Makes 4 servings.

Note: Any combination of seafood can be substituted for the chicken.

An elegant blend of seafood and yellow curry . . . perfect for guests.

THAI CRAB CURRY

2	pound cooked King crab
¼	cup oil
2	teaspoons Yellow Curry Paste (recipe page 125)
2	cups coconut milk
2 to 4	tablespoons fish sauce*
2	teaspoons brown sugar or honey
1 to 5	yellow chili peppers, seeded and chopped (optional)
3	green onions, cut into 2-inch lengths
	Hot steamed rice

Cut King crab into serving pieces. Leave shell on, but crack shell on each piece. In a saucepan heat oil and yellow curry paste on high heat, until curry paste bubbles. Add crab, coconut milk, fish sauce, brown sugar and yellow chili peppers; stir well and cook for about 7 minutes or until crab is heated through. Stir in green onions. Serve immediately. Accompany with hot steamed rice. Makes 6 servings.

*The amount of fish sauce used in this recipe depends on the brand selected and personal taste.

Fresh red chili peppers give this curry dish its heat, its flavor and its name.

RED PORK CURRY
(Illustrated on opposite page)

½	**pound lean pork**
2	**tablespoons oil**
1	**teaspoon Red Curry Paste (recipe page 126)**
½	**cup shredded young bamboo shoots**
3	**kaffir lime leaves**
1	**cup coconut milk**
10 to 15	**sweet basil leaves**
1 to 2	**tablespoons fish sauce***
1 to 5	**red chili peppers, chopped (optional)**
Garnish:	**Red chili peppers**
	Kaffir lime leaves
	Sweet basil leaves (optional)
	Hot steamed rice

Slice pork. In a saucepan heat oil and red curry paste on high heat, until curry paste bubbles. Add pork, bamboo shoots, kaffir lime leaves and coconut milk; stir well and cook for about 10 minutes or until pork is cooked. Mix in basil, fish sauce and red chili peppers. Garnish with red chili peppers, kaffir lime leaves and basil leaves. Serve immediately. Accompany with hot steamed rice. Makes 4 servings.

Idea: An excellent vegetarian curry can be prepared by substituting mixed vegetables for the pork. Use ½ teaspoon salt instead of the fish sauce.

*The amount of fish sauce used in this recipe depends on the brand selected and personal taste.

Left: Red Pork Curry (page 135)
Right: Green Shrimp Curry (page 136)

Eggplant, shrimp and coconut milk makes a nice combination. It's the green curry that makes it Thai's hottest!

GREEN SHRIMP CURRY

(Illustrated on page 134)

½	**pound fresh large shrimp**
2	**tablespoons oil**
1	**teaspoon Green Curry Paste (recipe page 127)**
1	**cup small and/or large Thai eggplant**
3	**kaffir lime leaves**
1	**stalk fresh lemon grass, thinly sliced**
1	**cup coconut milk**
10 to 15	**sweet basil leaves**
1 to 2	**tablespoons fish sauce***
1 to 5	**small green chili peppers, seeded and chopped (optional)**
Garnish:	**Kaffir lime leaves**
	Slices fresh lemon grass
	Sweet basil leaves (optional)
	Hot steamed rice

Rinse shrimp and devein. In a saucepan heat oil and green curry paste on high heat, until curry paste bubbles. Add shrimp, eggplant, kaffir lime leaves, lemon grass and coconut milk; stir well and cook for about 7 minutes or until shrimp are cooked. Mix in basil, fish sauce and green chili peppers. Garnish with kaffir lime leaves, slices fresh lemon grass and basil leaves. Serve immediately. Accompany with hot steamed rice. Makes 6 servings.

Note: Green peas can be substituted for Thai eggplant. Chicken can be substituted for the shrimp.

*The amount of fish sauce used in this recipe depends on the brand selected and personal taste.

This thick, dark, red curry with peanut butter is a flavorful combination with roast duck.

PANANG DUCK CURRY

(Illustrated on page 138 and 139)

1	**roast duck**
2	**tablespoons oil**
1	**teaspoon Regular (Musamun) Curry Paste (recipe page 124)**
1	**cup small Thai eggplant**
3	**kaffir lime leaves**
1	**cup coconut milk**
1	**tablespoon brown sugar**
2	**tablespoons peanut butter**
Garnish:	**Kaffir lime leaves (optional)**
	Hot steamed rice

Cut duck into serving pieces. In a saucepan heat oil and regular curry paste on high heat, until curry paste bubbles. Add duck, eggplant, kaffir lime leaves, coconut milk, brown sugar and peanut butter; stir well and cook for about 7 minutes or until heated through. Garnish with kaffir lime leaves. Serve immediately. Accompany with hot steamed rice. Makes 6 servings.

Note: Green peas can be substituted for the Thai eggplant. Chicken or beef can be substituted for the roast duck.

RICE AND NOODLES

Thai Noodles with Chicken — 143
Fried Noodles with Shrimp — 144
Thai Broccoli Noodles with Beef — 145
Steamed Rice — 148
Brown Rice — 148
Sticky Rice — 148
Water Chestnut Fried Rice — 149
Fried Rice with Beef — 151

One of the favorite dishes of Americans in Thailand. It is sold every-where from fine dining restaurants to sidewalk food stands.

THAI NOODLES WITH CHICKEN

(Illustrated on opposite page)

½	**pound rice noodles**
¼	**cup oil**
2	**cloves garlic, finely chopped**
1	**scant teaspoon shredded pickled salted radish**
¼	**pound boneless chicken breast, sliced**
1	**egg, lightly beaten**
½	**pound bean sprouts**
1	**tablespoon catsup**
1	**teaspoon soy sauce**
¼	**cup coarsely chopped peanuts or macadamia nuts**
1	**teaspoon sugar**
1 to 2	**tablespoons fish sauce***
1	**tablespoon dried ground salted shrimp optional)**
1	**ounce chives, cut into 2-inch lengths**
Garnish:	**Chinese parsley sprigs**
	1 lime, quartered
	1 teaspoon dried red chili pepper flakes (optional)

Soak rice noodles in warm water for 30 minutes; drain. Heat oil in a wok on high heat and cook garlic and salted radish until light brown. Add chicken and egg; stir fry for 3 to 4 minutes. Add rice noodles and half of the bean sprouts; mix well. Stir in catsup, soy sauce, peanuts, sugar, fish sauce and ground salted shrimp; cook for 3 minutes. Add chives and the remaining bean sprouts; mix well. Serve hot. Garnish with Chinese parsley, lime quarters and red chili pepper flakes. Sprinkle with extra chopped peanuts, if desired. Makes 3 to 4 servings.

*The amount of fish sauce used in this recipe depends on brand selected and personal taste.

This spicier version of Singapore noodles is quick and easy to prepare.

FRIED NOODLES WITH SHRIMP

1	**ounce rice noodles**
¼	**cup oil**
3	**cloves garlic, chopped**
6	**shallots, chopped**
¼	**pound fresh large shrimp, peeled and de-veined**
1	**onion, thinly sliced**
1	**egg, lightly beaten**
2 to 3	**tablespoons fish sauce***
1	**ounce chives, cut into 2-inch lengths**
¼	**teaspoon ground dried chili peppers (optional)**
3	**ounces bean sprouts**
Garnish:	**Chinese parsley sprigs**
	3 red chili peppers, thinly sliced
	1 lime, quartered

Soak rice noodles in warm water for 15 minutes; drain and cut into 4-inch lengths. In a skillet heat oil; add garlic and shallots and cook until light brown. Stir in shrimp, onion and egg and stir fry for 2 minutes, then reduce heat to medium. Stir in rice noodles, fish sauce, chives and ground dried chili peppers. Add bean sprouts; mix well and cook for 2 minutes. Serve immediately. Garnish with Chinese parsley, red chili peppers and lime. Makes 2 to 4 servings.

*The amount of fish sauce used in this recipe depends on the brand selected and personal taste.

Thin sliced beef with Asian broccoli and yellow bean sauce make this a good everyday dish.

THAI BROCCOLI NOODLES WITH BEEF

(Illustrated on pages 146 and 147)

¼	pound lean beef
6	tablespoons oil
½	pound fresh wide rice noodles
2	eggs (optional)
3	cloves garlic, finely chopped
1	pound broccoli (preferably Asian), cut into 2-inch lengths
1 to 3	teaspoons yellow bean sauce*
2	teaspoons oyster sauce

Thinly slice beef into 2-inch strips. Heat 2 tablespoons of the oil in a large wok on medium heat. Add rice noodles and eggs; mix well and cook for 2 minutes. Place rice noodles on a large serving platter; set aside. Heat the remaining 4 tablespoons of the oil on high heat in the same wok with garlic, until garlic is golden brown. Add beef, broccoli, yellow bean sauce and oyster sauce. Dissolve cornstarch in cold water and add to beef; stir well. Stir fry for 7 to 10 minutes. Pour broccoli mixture over noodles and serve immediately. Makes 2 to 4 servings.

Idea: Tofu, meat or seafood can be added to the recipe.

*Yellow bean sauce from Thailand is saltier than sauce from Hong Kong or China. Season to taste.

BROWN RICE

2½ cups brown rice
3 cups water
Salt to taste

Rinse rice in a colander until water runs clear; drain well. In a heavy saucepan with a tight fitting lid bring water and rice to a boil. Stir continuously until bubbles disappear from surface. Remove any scum. continue boiling until there is only a thin film of water covering the rice. Reduce heat to a simmer and cover with the lid. Cook for 10 to 15 minutes or until rice is tender. Remove from heat and fluff rice with a spatula. Cover for 5 more minutes. Serve hot. Makes 4 to 4½ cups.

STEAMED RICE

2½ cups long grain rice
3 cups water
Salt to taste

Rinse rice in a colander until water runs clear; drain well. In a heavy saucepan with a tight fitting lid bring water and rice to a boil. Stir continously until bubbles disappear from surface. Remove any scum. Continue boiling until there is only a thin film of water covering the rice. Reduce heat to a simmer and cover with the lid. Cook for 10 to 15 minutes or until rice is tender. Remove from heat and fluff rice with a spatula. Cover for 5 more minutes. Serve hot. Makes 5 to 6 cups.

STICKY RICE

1 cup sweet rice

Rinse rice in a colander until water runs clear; drain well. Place rice in a bowl and add water to cover. Let stand 12 hours or overnight. Drain. Spread rice in an even layer in a steamer lined with cheesecloth or in a sticky rice steaming basket. Cook, covered, over boiling water for 40 to 45 minutes or until tender and translucent. Remove from heat and fluff rice with a spatula. Serve hot. Makes 1½ cups.

Like Thai noodles, Thai style fried rice is served at any meal or as a snack. City folks like it better than villagers, however. A perfect dish for those who are vegetarians. The addition of pineapple chunks and shredded carrots give the dish color and a sweet-sour taste.

WATER CHESTNUT FRIED RICE

(Illustrated on page 150)

2	tablespoons oil
1	clove garlic, finely chopped
1	onion, thinly sliced
3	cups cooked rice
1	can (6 oz.) sliced water chestnuts
1	tomato, quartered
1	tablespoon tomato sauce
⅓	cup pineapple chunks (optional)
⅓	cup shredded carrots (optional)
½	teaspoon salt
1	cucumber, thinly sliced
Garnish:	Green onions,chopped
	Chinese parsley, cut into 2-inch lengths

In a wok heat oil on medium heat and cook garlic until light brown. Add onion and stir fry for 1 minute. Stir in rice, water chestnuts, tomato, tomato sauce, pineapple, carrots and salt; mix well and stir fry for 3 minutes. Serve with sliced cucumber. Garnish with green onions and Chinese parsley. Makes 4 servings.

This tasty dish is often served as a snack or can be a meal in itself.

FRIED RICE WITH BEEF

(Illustrated on page 150)

½	**pound beef**
2	**tablespoons oil**
1	**clove garlic, finely chopped**
1	**onion, thinly sliced**
1 to 2	**eggs, lightly beaten**
3	**cups cooked rice**
1	**tomato, quartered**
1	**tablespoon tomato sauce**
½ to 1	**tablespoon fish sauce***
1	**cucumber, thinly sliced**
Garnish:	**Green onions, chopped**
	Chinese parsley, cut into 2-inch lengths

Thinly slice beef into 2-inch strips. In a wok heat oil on medium heat and cook garlic until light brown. Stir in beef, onion and eggs. Increase heat to high and stir fry for 4 to 5 minutes or until beef is cooked. Add rice, tomato, tomato sauce and fish sauce and stir fry for 2 minutes. Serve with sliced cucumber. Garnish with green onions and Chinese parsley. Makes 6 servings.

Note: One half pound of shrimp, pork or chicken can be substituted for the beef.

*The amount of fish sauce used in this recipe depends on the brand selected and personal taste.

Clockwise from top left: Fried Rice with Shrimp, Fried Rice with Beef, and Water Chestnut Fried Rice (page 149)

DESSERTS

Mango with Sticky Rice — 156
Mango Bread — 157
Sticky Rice with Banana — 160
Fried Bananas with Rice Flour — 161
Thai Banana Chips — 161
Apple Banana with Coconut Milk — 162
Golden Threads Dessert — 163
Thai Tapioca Pudding — 166
Colorful Tapioca — 166
Steamed Pumpkin with Custard — 167

Fresh ripe mango slices and sticky rice lightly seasoned with coconut milk and sugar is a popular dessert in Thailand and Laos.

MANGO WITH STICKY RICE

(Illustrated on pages 154 and 155)

3 to 4	**ripe mangoes, chilled**
3	**cups cooked sticky rice**
1	**cup coconut milk**
2 to 4	**tablespoons sugar**
¼	**teaspoon salt**

Rinse mangoes and chill them whole. Peel and slice mangoes just before serving to keep the fresh sweet taste. In a saucepan combine sticky rice and coconut milk and cook on medium heat for 5 minutes or until thick. Stir in sugar and salt. The amount of sugar depends on the sweetness of the mangoes. Reduce heat to low and simmer, covered, for two minutes. Serve warm on a platter with chilled mango slices arranged around the edge. Makes 4 to 6 servings.

Exotic fresh fruit bread of excellent flavor.

MANGO BREAD

3	cups chopped mangoes
½	cup melted butter
3	eggs, lightly beaten
2	tablespoons molasses
¼	teaspoon vanilla
3	cups flour
2	teaspoons baking soda
1	tablespoon baking powder
½	teaspoon salt
½	cup shredded coconut
¼	cup chopped nuts (optional)

Preheat oven to 350F. Grease and flour two 3¼ x 9 x 5-inch loaf pans. In a large mixing bowl combine mangoes, butter, eggs, molasses and vanilla; mix well. Sift together flour, baking soda, baking powder and salt; blend into mango mixture. Lightly stir in coconut and nuts. Pour batter into prepared loaf pan and bake for 1 hour or until bread tests done. Makes 1 loaf.

A tasty dessert of apple banana strips and sticky wrice wrapped in banana leaves and steamed. Naturally good!

STICKY RICE WITH BANANA

(Illustrated on pages 158 and 159)

1	cup coconut milk
3	cups cooked sticky rice
¼	cup palm sugar
$\frac{1}{8}$	teaspoon salt
8 to 10	banana leaves, cut into 8-inch squares
3	ripe apple bananas, cut into 1-inch strips

In a saucepan combine coconut milk, sticky rice, palm sugar and salt. Cook on medium heat until thick. Place a layer, about 3 x 3 x ½-inch thick, of the rice mixture in the center of a banana leaf. Place a banana strip on the rice mixture, then wrap it up by lifting up two opposite sides of the banana leaf at a time, so the rice goes on top of the banana. Fold under the extra part of the leaf. Place in a steamer and steam for 25 minutes. Serve warm or cold. Makes 8 to 10 servings.

Clockwise from top center: Fried Bananas with Rice Flour (page 161), Sticky Rice with Bananas (page 160), Thai Banana Chips (page 161), and Apple Banana with Coconut Milk (page 162)

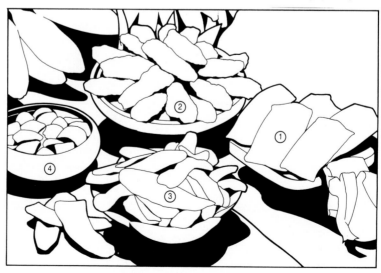

This children's favorite is from bananas coated with shredded coconut and rice flour, then deep fried. Crisp on the outside, soft and sweet inside.

FRIED BANANAS WITH RICE FLOUR

(Illustrated on pages 158 and 159)

8	firm ripe bananas
2	eggs, beaten
¼	cup sugar or honey
3	tablespoons rice flour
1	cup shredded coconut
¼	cup butter

Peel bananas and cut in half lengthwise, then in half crosswise. Combine eggs, sugar and rice flour; mix well. Dip bananas into egg mixture and coat generously. Roll in shredded coconut. Heat butter in a skillet and saute bananas for 10 minutes, turning once. Serve hot. Makes 8 servings.

Easy to make and keeps well for parties and picnics.

THAI BANANA CHIPS

(Illustrated on pages 158 and 159)

6	firm ripe apple bananas
1	cup lime juice
4	cups oil for deep frying
1	cup sugar

Peel bananas and slice very thin. Soak banana slices in lime juice for 10 to 15 minutes to prevent them from discoloring; rinse and drain well. Heat oil to 375F. and fry bananas until golden brown and crisp. Drain on absorbent paper. Roll in sugar. Makes 3 to 4 cups.

Apple banana slices cooked in fresh coconut milk is very popular in Thailand.

APPLE BANANA WITH COCONUT MILK

(Illustrated on pages 158 and 159)

12 half ripe apple bananas
4 cups fresh coconut milk
¼ cup palm sugar
$^1/_8$ teaspoon salt

Peel apple bananas and cut in quarters. Steam for 20 minutes; set aside. In a large pot heat coconut milk, palm sugar and salt on high heat and, as soon as it comes to a boil, add bananas. Reduce heat to a simmer and cook for 1 hour. Serve hot. Makes 6 servings.

The Thai name for this dessert is "foi tong". It is believed that the recipe came from Portuguese travelers in Thailand a couple of centuries ago. It is a favorite among the children, because it is so sweet.

GOLDEN THREADS DESSERT

24	**egg yolks (duck eggs preferred)**
3	**cups water**
4	**cups sugar**
Garnish:	**Shredded coconut**
Require:	**golden thread dispenser or an aluminum cone with a tip opening of $^1/_{12}$-inch**

In a large bowl beat egg yolks with an electric mixer or wire whip. In a wok bring water and sugar to a boil on high heat and cook until mixture becomes a syrup. Fill golden thread dispenser or aluminum cone with egg yolks, while holding the opening closed. Release opening over the boiling syrup and pipe egg yolks in a circular motion. As soon as dispenser is empty, scoop up all the cooked yolks and set aside. Refill dispenser and repeat above method until all yolks are used. Chill before serving. To serve, arrange in small individual portions and garnish with shredded coconut. Makes 6 to 8 servings.

Large pearl tapioca served warm with fresh coconut milk. Differs from American tapioca in that it is more on the liquid side and does not contain milk or eggs.

THAI TAPIOCA PUDDING

(Illustrated on pages 164 and 165)

⅓ **pound quick-cooking tapioca**
3 **cups water**
3 **tablespoons palm sugar or white sugar**
⅛ **teaspoon salt**
1 **cup coconut milk**

Rinse tapioca in cold water; drain and set aside. Bring water to a boil and stir in palm sugar and salt. Add tapioca and return to a boil. Stir in coconut milk. Reduce heat to a simmer. Stir frequently to prevent tapioca from sticking to the bottom of the pan. Cook for 30 minutes. Serve warm or cold. Makes 4 to 6 servings.

Waterchestnuts, tapioca flower and coconut milk make this a very interesting Thai dessert. Since it looks like pomegranate in color the Thai name for this dessert is "tap-tim-crob," meaning a crispy pomegranate.

COLORFUL TAPIOCA

(Illustrated on pages 164 and 165)

½ **pound waterchestnuts**
   Food coloring (red, green and yellow)
1 **cup tapioca flour**
6 **cups water**
2 **cups coconut milk**
½ **cup sugar or honey**

Peel waterchestnuts and dice into ¼-inch cubes. Divide waterchestnuts in four portions and dye three of the portions each a different color. Drain the waterchestnuts and toss them in tapioca flour to coat. In a large pot bring water to a boil. Add waterchestnuts to the water and bring to a second boil. Drain immediately; then chill in ice cold water. Combine coconut milk and sugar; blend well to dissolve sugar. Chill. Pour over tapioca to serve. Makes 4 to 6 servings.

Left: Colorful Tapioca (page 166)

Right: Tapioca Pudding (page 166)

Thais are very much into eating sweets. This is a very common Thai dessert using pumpkin, squash, young coconut or banana leaves filled with a coconut egg custard. Steam or bake.

STEAMED PUMPKIN WITH CUSTARD

3	**pumpkins (small enough to fit in a steamer)**
10	**eggs**
1	**cup coconut milk**
½	**cup palm sugar or brown sugar**
¹/₈	**teaspoon salt**

Cut tops off the pumpkins to form a hole 3-inches in diameter. Remove seeds and rinse out pumpkins. Combine eggs, coconut milk, palm sugar and salt; blend well. Fill pumpkins with the egg mixture. Replace tops. Steam for 30 to 45 minutes or until the egg mixture is of a cooked custard consistency. Chill. Makes 4 servings.

BEVERAGES

Thai Iced Coffee — 171
Thai Iced Tea — 171
Guava Daiquiri — 172
Lychee Shake — 172
Lilikoi Float — 173
Evil Princess — 173
Mango Daiquiri — 175

THAI ICED COFFEE

¼   **cup strong French roasted coffee**
½   **cup boiling water**
2   **teaspoons sweetened condensed milk**
     Ice cubes

Combine coffee, boiling water and sweetened condensed milk; stir until blended. Pour into 2 tall glasses filled with ice cubes. Makes 2 servings.

THAI ICED TEA

(Illustrated on opposite page)

¼   **cup strong Thai tea**
½   **cup boiling water**
2   **teaspoons sweetened condensed milk**
     Ice cubes
Garnish: Mint leaves

Combine Thai tea, boiling water and sweetened condensed milk; stir until blended. Pour into 2 tall glasses filled with ice cubes. Garnish with mint leaves. Makes 2 servings.

GUAVA DAIQUIRI

2 ounces light rum
2 ounces guava juice concentrate
1 tablespoon fresh lime juice
1 teaspoon sugar
   Dash of grenadine
   Scoop of cracked ice

Combine rum, guava juice concentrate, lime juice, sugar and grenadine in a blender. Blend on high speed for 30 seconds. Gradually add cracked ice, blending until drink is of a slushy consistency. Makes 2 drinks. An excellent before or after dinner drink.

LYCHEE SHAKE

2 scoops lychee sherbet
2 cups milk

Combine lychee sherbet and milk in a blender. Blend on high speed until smooth. Makes 2 servings.

Note: Coconut, mango, banana, guava or lilikoi (passion fruit) sherbet can be substituted for the lychee sherbet.

LILIKOI FLOAT

> **2 scoops lilikoi (passion fruit) sherbet**
> **2 cups chilled lemon-lime soda**

In a tall glass combine lilikoi sherbet and lemon-lime soda. Stir with a long spoon until well mixed. Makes 2 servings.

Note: Mango, guava or coconut sherbet can be substituted for the lilikoi sherbet.

An excellent before or after dinner drink. A Keo's original!

EVIL PRINCESS

> **2 ounces light rum**
> **2 cups seeded and sliced fresh jackfruits**
> **2 ounces pineapple juice**
> **2 ounces orange juice**
> **1 ounce coconut milk**
> **Scoop of cracked ice**

Combine rum, jackfruit, pineapple juice, orange juice and coconut milk in a blender. Blend on high speed for 30 seconds. Gradually add cracked ice, blending until drink is of a slushy consistency. Makes 2 to 3 servings.

MANGO DAIQUIRI

(Illustrated on opposite page)

2 ounces light rum
1 large ripe mango, peeled and seeded
1 tablespoon fresh lemon juice
1 teaspoon sugar (optional)
   Scoop of cracked ice

Combine rum, mango, lemon juice and sugar in a blender. Blend on high speed for 30 seconds. Gradually add cracked ice, blending until drink is of a slushy consistency. Makes 2 drinks.

GARNISH IDEAS and TECHNIQUES

Tomato Lotus Flower — 178
Red Chili Flower — 179
Cucumber Fan — 180
Folded Cucumber — 181
Cucumber Leaves — 182
Green Onion Brush — 183
Technique for Wrapping Spring Rolls — 184
Technique for Deboning Chicken Wings — 185
Technique for Cleaning and Scoring Squid — 186

TOMATO LOTUS FLOWER

Place a tomato stem end down. Starting at the bottom of the tomato make cuts through the skin 1-inch apart to form petals. In the middle of each petal cut a smaller petal. Slowly peel the outer petal back to form a tomato lotus flower.

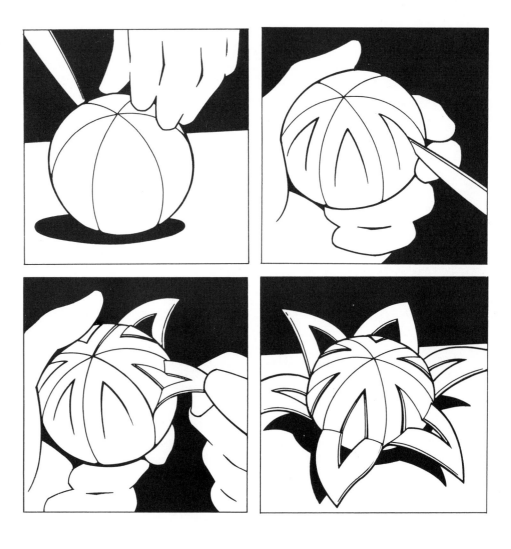

RED CHILI FLOWER

Trim off the tip of a red chili pepper. Cut chili pepper lengthwise with scissors to form petals. Trim the tip of each petal to a point. Remove seeds. Soak in ice water for 5 minutes or until red chili flower opens up.

CUCUMBER FAN

Slice a cucumber in half lengthwise, then cut on the diagonal into sections 2-inches in length. Cut a number of notches along the top of each cucumber section. Make a series of thin cuts down to within ½-inch of the end of each cucumber section. Fan cucumber open by gently pressing down.

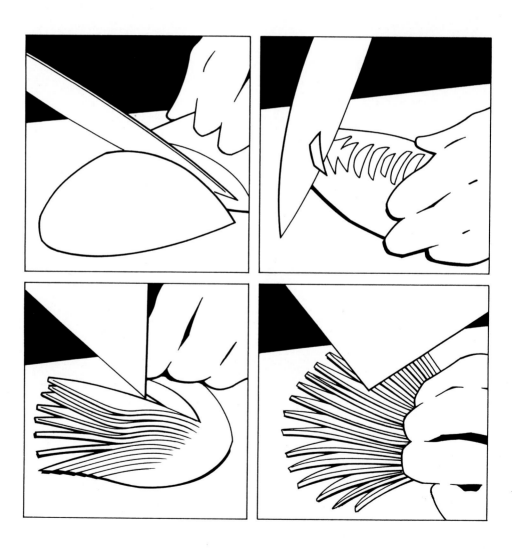

FOLDED CUCUMBER

Slice a cucumber in half lengthwise, then cut on the diagonal into sections 1-inch in length. Make six thin cuts down to within ½-inch of the opposite side of each cucumber section. Soak in salt water (1 tablespoon salt to 1 quart of water) for 15 minutes to make the skin pliable. Tuck under every other cut until you have 3 folded down.

CUCUMBER LEAVES

Slice off long thick strips from a cucumber. Cut notches on both sides of the strips to resemble a leaf. Etch a thick center vein and thin lines to represent small veins coming out from the center vein. Place cucumber leaves in ice water until ready to use.

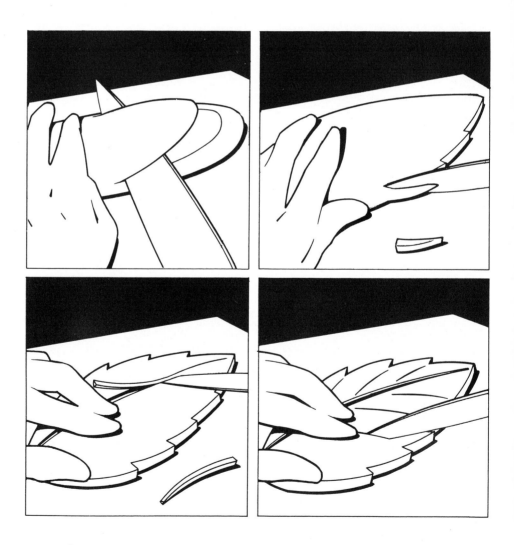

GREEN ONION BRUSH

Cut off the root end of a green onion and cut into 2-inch lengths. Insert the point of a needle ½-inch from the end and pull up through the green onion. Repeat this step all the way around the green onion. Soak in ice water for 5 minutes or until green onion brush curls.

TECHNIQUE FOR WRAPPING SPRING ROLLS

Cut rice paper circles into quarters. Place rice paper on a flat surface and brush with water until pliable. Place 2 teaspoons of filling near the edge. Fold rice paper over the filling. Fold the right side over to enclose filling, then fold over left side. Roll tightly and seal.

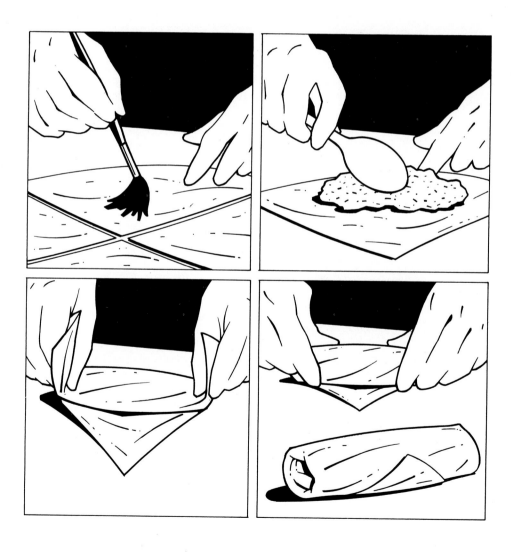

TECHNIQUE FOR DEBONING CHICKEN WINGS

Cut off top portion of chicken wing and reserve for other use. Cut through joint to separate two bones. Push meat gently down bones and twist or cut through tendon at base of bones and remove them. Stuff mixture into pocket.

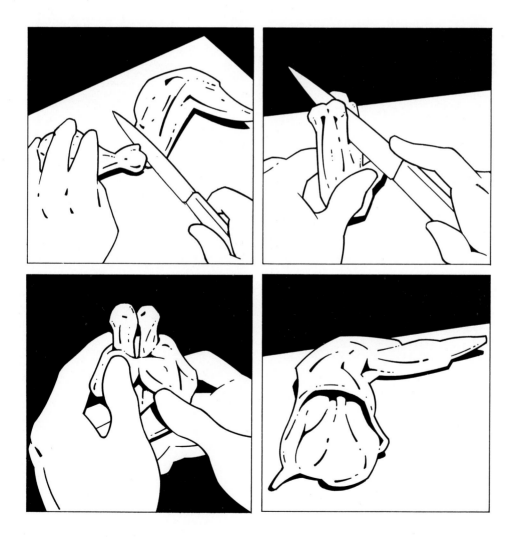

TECHNIQUE FOR CLEANING AND SCORING SQUID

Grasp the squid gently but firmly with both hands and pull the mantle away from the head. Pull the pen (tail skeleton) from the inside of the mantle and discard it. Peel off the thin skin. Rinse the mantle under running cold water and remove the remaining innards. Cut into 2-inch sections. Slit the sections open and lay them on a flat surface. Lightly score the squid on the diagonal in a crosshatch pattern every ¼-inch.

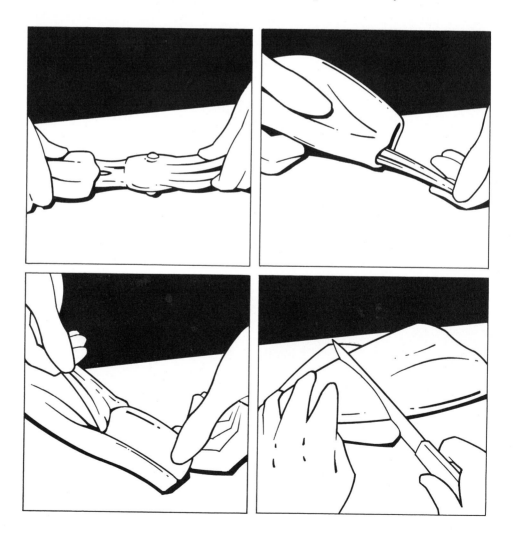

THAI EATING HABITS

Chopsticks are used only when noodles are served in Thai homes or restaurants. Most Thais eat with a fork and a spoon. The spoon held in the right hand carries the food while the fork is held in the left hand and is used to push food onto the spoon. In the villages or on informal occasions the spoon and fingers are acceptable, especially when sticky rice is served. The meals are served family style which allows you to taste everything served on the table.

Thais enjoy eating and drinking. When not eating, it is normal to discuss plans for the next meal. There are no restrictions on food or beverage in Thailand. Buddhist restrictions on taking life do not prevent Thais from eating meat and even the monks and nuns eat meat when they are served by the people.

There are food vendors everywhere in Thailand selling little snacks or full meal menus. The English version of thai menus in most restaurants in Thailand may be a bit strange for foreigners, such items such as Lady's Fingers Salad, Cow Pad, Horse's Urine Eggs, Mouse's Droppings Chili, Metallic Manures Soup. It is perfectly okay to ask about items unfamiliar or to refuse something which is served to you when you are a guest in Thailand.

MENU SUGGESTIONS

for 2 Crisp Fried Tofu
Green Papaya Salad
Sa-teh Shrimp
Water Chestnut Fried Rice

for 4 Fish Patties
Spicy Shrimp Soup with Lemon Grass
Thai Beef Salad
Cashew Chicken
Green Shrimp Curry
Steamed Rice
Tapioca Pudding

for 6 Crisp Noodles
Thai Ginger Chicken Soup
Calamari Salad with Fresh Lemon Grass
Thai Shrimp with Garlic
Beef with Fresh Sweet Basil
Panang Duck
Brown Rice
Mango with Sticky Rice

for 8 Keo's Thai Spring Rolls
Spicy Shrimp Soup with Lemon Grass
Chieng Mai Chicken Salad
Whole Fish with Fresh Ginger and
 Yellow Bean Sauce
Beef with Oyster Sauce
Evil Jungle Prince with Mixed Vegetables
Sticky Rice
Brown Rice
Apple Banana with Coconut Milk

INDEX

A

Appetizer
Bangkok Stuffed Wings - 23
Crispy Fried Chicken - 27
Crisp Fried Crab Claws - 26
Crisp Fried Tofu - 33
Crisp Noodles - 21
Fish Patties - 18
Keo's Thai Spring Rolls - 17
Salted Eggs - 31
Sa-teh on Skewers - 29
Shrimp Rolls - 19
Son-In-Law Eggs - 30
Stuffed Tofu - 22

Asparagus
Asparagus with Black Mushrooms - 115
Asparagus with Shrimp and Black Mushrooms - 63

B

Banana
Apple Banana with Coconut Milk - 162
Fried Bananas with Rice Flour - 161
Sticky Rice with Banana - 160
Thai Banana Chips - 161

Beef
Beef with Fresh Sweet Basil - 101
Beef with Oyster Sauce - 104
Beef with String Beans and Fresh Ginger - 100
Crispy Fried Beef - 105
Fried Rice with Beef - 151
Musamun Beef Curry - 131
Rice Soup - 42
Sa-teh on Skewers - 29
Thai Beef Salad - 53
Thai Broccoli Noodles with Beef - 145
Thai Noodle Soup with Beef Meatballs - 45

Beverage
Evil Princess - 173
Guava Daiquiri - 172
Lilikoi Float - 173
Lychee Shake - 172
Mango Daiquiri - 175
Thai Iced Coffee - 171
Thai Iced Tea - 171

C

Chicken
Bangkok Stuffed Wings - 23
Bar-B-Que Chicken - 89
Cashew Chicken - 99
Chieng Mai Chicken Salad - 51
Chicken with Black Mushrooms - 97
Chicken with Fresh Sweet Basil - 88
Crisp Noodles - 21
Crispy Fried Chicken - 27
Eggplant with Chicken - 95
Evil Jungle Prince with Chicken - 92
Sa-teh on Skewers - 29
Thai Chicken Soup with Bean Threads - 43
Thai Ginger Chicken Soup - 38
Thai Noodle Soup with Chicken - 47
Thai Noodles with Chicken - 143
Thai Soup Stock - 39
Yellow Chicken Curry - 132

Clam
Steamed Clams with Fresh Ginger - 85

Crab
Crab Legs with Yellow Bean Sauce - 76
Crisp Fried Crab Claws - 26
Shrimp Rolls - 19
Stuffed Crab - 87
Thai Crab Curry - 133

Curry Paste
Green Curry Paste - 127
Red Curry Paste - 126
Regular (Musamun) Curry Paste - 124
Yellow Curry Paste - 125

D

Dessert
  Apple Banana with Coconut Milk - 162
  Colorful Tapioca - 166
  Fried Bananas with Rice Flour - 161
  Golden Threads Desserts - 163
  Mango Bread - 157
  Mango with Sticky Rice - 156
  Steamed Pumpkin with Custard - 167
  Sticky Rice with Banana - 160
  Tapioca Pudding - 166
  Thai Banana Chips - 161

Duck
  Panang Duck Curry - 137
  Roast Duck with Chili - 96
  Thai Roast Duck - 92

E

Eggplant
  Eggplant with Chicken - 95
  Eggplant with Tofu - 110
  Green Shrimp Curry - 136
  Panang Duck Curry - 137

Eggs
  Fried Bananas with Rice Flour - 161
  Golden Threads Dessert - 163
  Mango Bread - 157
  Salted Eggs - 31
  Son-In-Law Eggs - 30
  Steamed Pumpkin with Custard - 167

F

Fish
  Fish Patties - 18
  Opakapaka with Red Curry Sauce - 73
  Steamed Fish Eggs with Dill - 68
  Thai Sweet and Sour Fish - 69
  Whole Fish with Fresh Ginger and Yellow Bean Sauce - 72

L

Lobster
  Lobster with Pineapple - 77

Long Rice (Bean Threads)
  Bangkok Stuffed Wings - 23
  Calamari Salad with Fresh Lemon Grass - 55
  Keo's Thai Spring Rolls - 17
  Stuffed Crab - 87
  Thai Beef Salad - 53
  Thai Chicken Soup with Bean Threads — 43

M

Mango
  Mango Bread - 157
  Mango with Sticky Rice - 156

Mussels
  Fried Mussels with Fresh Whole Chili Peppers - 84

N

Noodles
  Crisp Noodles - 21
  Egg Noodle Soup with Char Siu - 46
  Fried Noodles with Shrimp - 144
  Thai Broccoli Noodles with Beef - 145
  Thai Noodle Soup with Beef Meatballs - 45
  Thai Noodle Soup with Chicken - 47
  Thai Noodles with Beef - 145
  Thai Noodles with Chicken - 143

P

Pork
  Egg Noodle Soup with Char Siu - 46
  Keo's Thai Spring Rolls - 17
  Red Pork Curry - 135
  Sa-teh on Skewers - 29

R

Rice
Brown Rice - 148
Fried Rice with Beef - 151
Mango with Sticky Rice - 156
Rice Soup - 42
Steamed Rice - 148
Sticky Rice - 148
Sticky Rice with Banana - 160
Water Chestnut Fried Rice - 149

S

Salad
Calamari Salad with Fresh Lemon Grass - 55
Chieng Mai Chicken Salad - 51
Cucumber Salad - 52
Green Papaya Salad - 57
Thai Beef Salad - 53
Young Green Tamarind Salad - 56

Sauce
Cucumber Sauce - 121
Sa-teh Sauce - 119
Spring Roll Sauce - 120
Thai Curry Sauce - 127

Scallops
Scallops with Fresh Basil - 80

Shrimp
Asparagus with Shrimp and Black Mushrooms - 63
Bangkok Stuffed Wings - 23
Crisp Noodles - 21
Fried Noodles with Shrimp - 144
Green Shrimp Curry - 136
Keo's Thai Spring Rolls - 17
Sa-teh Shrimp - 67
Shrimp Rolls - 19
Shrimp with Mixed Vegetables - 81
Shrimp with Red Chili Paste - 65
Spicy Shrimp Soup with Lemon Grass - 37
Stuffed Crab - 87
Thai Shrimp with Garlic - 19

Soup
Egg Noodle Soup with Char Siu - 46
Rice Soup - 42
Spicy Shrimp Soup with Lemon Grass - 37
Thai Chicken Soup with Bean Threads - 43
Thai Ginger Chicken Soup - 38
Thai Noodle Soup with Beef Meatballs - 45
Thai Noodle Soup with Chicken - 47
Thai Soup Stock - 39

String Beans
Beef with String Beans and Fresh Ginger - 100
String Beans with Fresh Ginger - 109

T

Tamarind
Crisp Noodles - 21
Sa-teh Shrimp - 67
Sa-teh Sauce - 119
Young Green Tamarind Salad - 56

Tofu
Crisp Fried Tofu - 33
Eggplant with Tofu - 110
Shrimp Rolls - 19

V

Vegetables
Asparagus with Black Mushrooms - 115
Eggplant with Tofu - 110
Evil Jungle Prince with Mixed Vegetables - 113
Shrimp with Mixed Vegetables - 81
Stir Fried Ong Choi with Yellow Bean Sauce - 111
String Beans with Fresh Ginger - 109
Thai Sweet and Sour Fish - 69
Thai Sweet and Sour Vegetables - 114